D0850434

Phonics Exposed

Understanding and Resisting Systematic Direct Intense Phonics Instruction

Phonics Exposed

Understanding and Resisting Systematic Direct Intense Phonics Instruction

Richard J. Meyer
University of New Mexico

 LAWRENCE ERLBAUM ASSOCIATES, PUBLISHERS
2002   Mahwah, New Jersey   London

Lawrence Erlbaum Associates, Inc., Publishers
10 Industrial Avenue
Mahwah, New Jersey 07430

Cover design by Kathryn Houghtaling Lacey

Cover art by Patricia S. Meyer

Library of Congress Cataloging-in-Publication Data

Meyer, Richard J., 1949–
    Phonics exposed : understanding and resisting systematic direct intense phonics
    instruction / Richard J. Meyer.
        p.   cm.
    Includes bibliographical references and indexes.
    ISBN 0-8058-3910-0 (cloth) — ISBN 0-8058-3911-9 (pbk.)
        1. Reading—Phonetic method—United States—Case studies.   2. English
    language—Phonetics—Programmed instruction—Case studies.   I. Title.
    LB1573.3 .M49   2001
    372.46'5—dc21   00-067728
                                                                         CIP

Books published by Lawrence Erlbaum Associates are printed on acid-free paper,
and their bindings are chosen for strength and durability.

Printed in the United States of America
10 9 8 7 6 5 4 3 2 1

*For Pat, who lives the life of a
writer's widow, like a rock.*

Contents

Foreword

Yetta M. Goodman
The University of Arizona

Once again the American public is faced with a phonics debate. Newspapers are filled with sensational headlines babbling about *Reading Wars*. The same statistics are used by some to prove that American children read well and by others to decry the low reading scores of American children in world comparisons. The answer to the mythology of reading problems is, for some at the present time, the explicit teaching of phonics: the "chicken soup" of reading instruction that will obviously solve the ills of illiteracy in society through commercially published programs. The superiority of phonics as the sole successful method to teach reading and the failure of all other methods raises its ugly head every 10 or 15 years. In my 50 years of experience in professional education, this is the fourth round. I remember in the 1950s the concern about why Johnny wasn't reading. The response was an attempt to make teachers give up successful integrated language curricula developed by teachers in which students learned to read and write as they explored social studies and science concepts. In the 1960s, I sat in inner-city classrooms in Detroit, Michigan, supervising student teachers who were teaching children to blend and "say it fast" for 2½ hours a day. A decade later in Tucson, Arizona, I observed student teachers preparing as many as nine ditto sheets that had to be completed before 11:00 a.m. by two groups of children working silently as a third group worked with the teacher on work attack and recognition skills. And then after hundreds of thousands of children suffered through boring reading programs, endless worksheets focused on abstract units of language, and numerous ends of level tests, the same groups of children were still not succeeding on standardized tests designed with a one-size-fits-all mentality. Once again, teachers, teacher educators, and reading specialists were able to take control of and organize integrated and holistic curricula to help students not only learn to read but also discover the joy and significance of reading.

Throughout these years of the tensions between reading methodologies, books, articles, and monographs were written to explore the most beneficial reading instruction, the reasons for the cyclical return to a focus on phonics promoted by specific researchers, publishers, politicians, and parents. However, little has been written about the impact that mandated commercially published phonics programs have on those most affected: teachers and children in classrooms. This is the focus Richard Meyer's *Phonics Exposed* takes. "There is a dearth of writing about how mandated phonics programs influence the learning and teaching lives of those who are in schools every day of the school year," he writes, and then makes it abundantly clear that reading is political. He demonstrates how the impositions of mandates and laws about the teaching of reading deprofessionalizes the art and science of teaching reading and at the same time disenfranchises children from becoming critical and life-long readers. In response, I want to explore two issues that are most important to me: the role of classroom teachers in curriculum development and the significance of academic freedom and decision making in democratic public schools.

THE ROLE OF THE CLASSROOM TEACHER

The readers of this book are introduced to Karen, a teacher being forced to give up her professional knowledge and successful teaching practices in favor of a commercial phonics program developed by people who know much less than she does about teaching children and the teaching of reading. We become aware of how teacher expertise is set aside and how children's cultural, racial, academic, and geographic regional differences become invisible as everything is subsumed under a single commercial program. Fine teachers like Karen have always been able to organize a classroom rich in experiences, taking into account the home, community, and school backgrounds of their children. These teachers know about kidwatching and child development. They are knowledgeable about the reading process and reading instruction. They use their professional sense to build on children's construction of knowledge to teach phonics, grammar, and meaning making to support their reading development. They know that reading and writing develop best as children are involved in learning about their world, using written language to explore significant themes in the social and physical sciences as well as the arts and humanities.

We live in a time when teachers are more knowledgeable than ever before. They participate in study groups, take courses to obtain advanced degrees, join professional organizations in which they are active, and research their students' reading abilities and their own reading instruction. But in the present climate, the richness of teacher knowledge and classroom experiences is narrowed. The uniqueness of teachers and students becomes insignificant in the wake of a published reading program that promises results that will ultimately not be forthcoming.

DEMOCRACY AND ACADEMIC FREEDOM

I taught during the McCarthy period when teachers were afraid. They were afraid to teach about the United Nations. They were afraid to make even neutral statements about the Soviet Union. Because of our fear we stayed away from controversy. I was drawn back to those oppressive times as I read about the fears of experienced teachers to respond articulately to administrators and boards of education about their tampering with the reading curriculum.

In democratic classrooms, teachers negotiate curriculum with their students: They understand how to honor state guidelines and at the same time respect the needs of each student. They know how to use textbooks and trade books in ways that help students question what they read. They know how to support children in learning to read as they are reading to learn. It is difficult to establish a democratic curriculum in an atmosphere of fear. How is teaching for democracy possible if commercial reading programs must be used and followed without question?

Public education has been at the forefront of American democracy where families from all walks of life come together to learn and grow. I agree with Dr. Meyer that the issues raised over the years about phonics and the teaching of reading are not the real reason for the debates. Rather what is under attack is public education itself. The hidden motive underlying the attacks is to prove the failure of public education and as a result to move toward privatization.

I wish teachers and teacher educators would rise up en masse, march to the state capitols, and sit in at school board meetings to make clear that they will not follow mandates without question; that they demand to be treated like the professionals that they are; and that public education needs to be protected. However, the teaching profession in the United States is not comfortable reacting so radically. But there are other ways to articulate our concerns. *Phonics Exposed* is not only an exposé of the phonics debacle but is just as importantly a call to action. If we do not act, we send the message that we agree with the focus on phonics and that we accept the myth that American public schools have failed. We have to relate the attack on phonics to attacks on affirmative action, bilingual education, and the lack of funding for public education, especially in the schools of the poorest of our citizens. We need to discuss how single methodologies, textbooks, standardized tests, and leveled books control teachers and constrain children's learning to read. We need to document the rich experiences children have in classrooms when literacy is used for democratic purposes. We can write books, articles, letters to the editor, and opinion pieces. We can organize forums in schools and libraries. We must articulate clearly that answers to educational problems are not in the control of curriculum and teachers by outside forces. Rather, in freeing professional teachers to use their expertise we support the literacy development of all children.

Preface

> *In our quest for higher standards and superior academic perform-*
> *ance, we seem to have forgotten that schools cannot be excellent as*
> *long as there are groups of children who are not well served by them.*
> —Jeannie Oakes in *Keeping Track* (1985, p. xiv).

There are many books, research reports, and articles being written in what
seems to be the never-ending debate over the role of phonics in the teaching of reading. There are writings on how to use phonics, why to use phonics, when to use phonics, and who needs phonics. There are critiques from
all sides and angles. There are passionate pleas, moving anecdotes of success and failure, and most important, suggestions and intimations about
what is going on in classrooms. Many of these reports cite large numbers of
students, many teachers, and dismal numbers. Teachers are portrayed as in-
competent, and students are portrayed as not learning to read.

One consistently missing piece of all of the pictures being painted is a
close-up view of phonics instruction—at the chalkface and near the children. No one gets intimate with the lives of children and their teacher
when a mandated phonics program is institutionalized in a school district.
No one has studied the impact of systematic (which means having a strict
set of rules to teach and a rigid sequence), direct (which means delivered
to students with little interaction or transaction; Rosenblatt, 1978), intense
(which means occurring for long periods of time daily, no matter what else
students need or can do) phonics (which means focused on letter–sound
relationships) instruction on students and a teacher in a classroom. No one
until now, that is.

This study began as a research project investigating predictable texts
and the ways teachers use them to support children's learning to read.
When the study began, the district held teachers in fairly high esteem and

trusted them to make decisions that were good for children, teaching, and learning. As the study progressed, the district yielded to pressures to have a systematic direct intense phonics program. The texts of that program began to dominate classrooms. Interestingly, the publishers claimed that the texts in the program were decodable and predictable (so the research continued), although some teachers reported that the texts were quite difficult for children to read despite the regularity of spelling and sounds. It becomes clear in this book that it is more difficult to read (and understand) "Dan has a pal" than it is to read and understand "Dan has a friend." Kids don't see or hear *pal* very much and tend to become word callers rather than readers when they are stuck in texts about pals, ham, can, and cats. The study continued to look at predictable texts in classrooms, focusing on what the district and publishers were calling *predictable texts*.

In this book, you will meet Karen and her students during a phonics lesson. After a brief introduction in chapter 1 about why I chose to write a book on phonics, I present a real-life phonics lesson, in chapter 2, as it occurred in Karen's classroom. This typical lesson, following the script of the program, is the cornerstone of the book. I wrote it as a play-by-play of the lesson so that as you read it you'll see it as a movie in your mind.

You'll come to know Karen and some of her students as the lesson and the book proceed. Imagine the phonics lesson (chap. 2) as the center of the book. Each subsequent chapter is a way of analyzing the lesson. In chapter 3, I analyze the phonics lesson by considering the definition of reading that is presented (implicitly) in the lesson. I offer a way (Appendix) for you to think about how important phonics rules are and how you use them as a reader and a teacher of reading. In chapter 4, I discuss the idea and place of teacher knowledge as it relates to the lesson. I consider what skills a teacher has and needs to use in a lesson that is completely scripted.

Chapter 5 closely looks at the children, and their roles and positions during the lesson, and considers what they are learning in the lesson. Chapter 6 is a discussion of curriculum—where it comes from, who it serves, how it serves, and what it is for. Again, this is viewed from the phonics lesson. Chapter 7 is a discussion of the role of culture in the lesson. Cultural differences and culturally relevant pedagogy are considered as they relate to the scripted phonics lesson. In chapter 8, I discuss the ways in which everything we do in schools is political. I know that many teachers don't like this idea, and I admit that when I went into teaching I never thought I was doing political work. I now know that I am, have been, and always will be political. I know that scripted lessons are political action; resistance to them is also political work. These ideas are presented in

greater depth in this chapter. Finally, chapter 9 presents ways in which
teachers (and supporters of teachers) can act to maintain academic freedom expressed as professional decision making in classrooms.

This book is a roller coaster of sorts. I present the difficulty that a
teacher encounters in a phonics lesson. I present children who are confused and frustrated. Yet I constantly present hope in the forms of smart
teachers, curious children, and possibilities for action.

The book is an exposé of sorts. It seems so necessary to get into classrooms, up close and personal, to see how programs like the one used by
Karen influence and affect children's learning and teachers' teaching. But
no one has. At least no one I can find. It is time to tell the story of these
programs from the children's and teachers' points of view. It is time to expose what the programs are doing to the precious spaces for teaching and
learning that our schools are supposed to be for.

ACKNOWLEDGMENTS

I've had so much help with this book from wonderful teachers and their
students, but I will not name them. I hope they know who they are and understand that in the present climate I do not feel comfortable naming them.

The reviewers of this book provided many ideas for changes that make
the book more readable and consistent. Prisca Martens' knowledge of
children's lives, their reading, and their writing helped me clarify my presentation of the children. Kathy Whitmore's understanding of what teachers and literacy researchers expect in a book of this nature led to more consistent and less redundant text. Alan Flurkey's thoughts about the reading
process helped me think about reading, curriculum, and the political nature of the decisions teachers make. My mentor, teacher, and friend, Yetta
Goodman, has influenced my thinking in ways that have enriched my life
and, hopefully, the lives I touch.

Ruth Luckasson, my colleague at the University of New Mexico,
helped me explore and understand some of the special education literature
on frustration and communicative intent. Her patience and assistance in
locating sources saved me countless hours of work in dusty library stacks.

Naomi Silverman's constant faith in me, wonderful phone messages,
and conversations rekindled my inspiration when it began to wane.
Barbara Wieghaus' help with production is also appreciated.

Many graduate students at the University of New Mexico listened to
drafts of various parts of this book. I thank them for their critique and discussions.

Many times during the writing of this book, I thought of my friend, Geane Hanson, whose gentle ways helped me *imaginate* the possibilities.

And, my family tolerated my absence as I disappeared into the manuscript of this book. Thank you, Sadie, Zoe, and Pat.

I am so grateful to Pat Meyer, for spending hours designing the cover of this book.

—*Richard J. Meyer*

1

Why Another Book on Phonics?

I was told by [the district reading administrator] that for too long teachers in this district have thought that their job was to create curriculum. I was told that is not our job. Our job is to "deliver" [she makes quote signs in the air with her fingers] curriculum . . . we are not allowed to think for ourselves or make decisions.

—Karen, a primary teacher

THE SMEAR CAMPAIGN

I never thought that I would be writing a book about phonics. I've grown weary, along with other teachers and learners, of the supposed war between phonics and whole language (Carbo, 1988; Chall, 1989; Taylor, 1989) because I'm convinced that it's not a war at all; it's more of a smear campaign that seems ultimately directed at hurting teachers and students while supporting the publishers of the phonics programs (see Berliner & Biddle, 1995; Spring, 1997; Taylor, 1998). That smear campaign is one motivation for writing this book.

Every teacher of reading (which is every teacher in every classroom) had better be teaching phonics. Although accusations are made about whole language teachers in particular as not teaching phonics, there is no whole language without phonics because phonics is one of the cueing systems that readers use to make meaning as they read.

However, it's not the only cueing system, and children need many and varied experiences with print to become proficient readers. Ken Goodman (1993), often *wrongly* accused of suggesting that teachers should not teach phonics, wrote a book about phonics, in which he discussed the ways in which readers use phonics as they make sense of text. So why another book about phonics? Because the smear campaign is working: Teachers' judgments are being devalued and students' lives in schools are becoming increasingly joyless.

As the debates rage in various professional literatures, research journals, in the popular press, in legislatures, and even in some houses of worship, districts are responding by adopting phonics programs. The programs make unsubstantiated claims (Coles, 2000; Taylor, 1998) about teaching reading to children in primary grades (kindergarten—or even prekindergarten—through third grade) and particularly for children whose first language is not English or who come from lower socioeconomic families. Although books are available to teachers on how to teach phonics effectively, based on research and with sensitivity toward differences (Hornsby, Parry, & Sukarna, 1992; Moustafa, 1997; D. Strickland, 1998), these are set aside when districts adopt programs and inform teachers that they must follow prescribed scripted lessons in the sequences dictated in the teachers' guides from the publishers. There is little research on many of the programs (Allington, 1997), yet they are being adopted.

The programs are being instituted with such zeal that teachers refer to various administrators as "phonics police," "phonics patrol," or "curriculum cops." The debates may continue for years, yet districts are responding as if the debates have ended and the overwhelming victors certainly appear to be the publishers. The spoils of their victories are profits in millions of dollars. Still, a question lingers in the minds of my friends and colleagues, as well as research partners who are some of the children and teachers in the classrooms in which these programs land. The question is this: *Is the phonics program that my district has adopted good for students?*

This question demands a book on phonics. The question begs at the phonics issue, but not in a "once and for all" end to some manufactured and senseless search for THE ONE RIGHT WAY to teach reading. The question demands another book on phonics because there seems to be a dearth of writing about how such phonics programs influence the learning and teaching lives of those who are in schools every day of the school year. To put it simply, no one seems to be looking at the children and teachers in schools where such programs are being adopted.

No one is looking at and asking questions about how programs that are advertised as good for all students change the reading lives of children in schools. No one is looking at and asking questions about what happens to the role of the professional teacher as a decision maker when she or he is required to teach from a script. In this book, I look closely and ask.

MANUFACTURING TEACHERS' ANGER
AND SELF-DOUBT

The issues of phonics program effectiveness, the directions that school districts have been taking, and a myriad of questions about lives in schools were rolling around my mind when Karen invited me, a professor at a local university, to observe her teaching of the district's mandated phonics program in her primary level classroom. The mandated phonics program was a dramatic shift in district policy. Prior to the mandate, primary teachers in the district were being encouraged and supported in the use of developmentally appropriate practices. "Developmentally appropriate practices" is a term used to denote curriculum that is based on the needs and interests of children, informal observations made by teachers, and the use of materials and strategies that children find engaging (Bredekamp, 1987). The district's early childhood administrator was an active member of the National Association for the Education of Young Children (NAEYC), and she invited me to engage in research and professional development in the district. She and I worked together to help teachers form study groups as a form of sustained professional development focused on literacy, inquiry, and developmentally appropriate practice. I was involved in study groups and made numerous presentations throughout the district. Through this work, I met outstanding teachers like Karen. I studied their uses of predictable texts, initially within the context of their developmentally appropriate classrooms and later in the context of their publisher-controlled classrooms.

The shift that occurred away from developmentally appropriate practice was brought about by the publication in the local newspaper of the district's *supposedly* declining second-grade test scores. I write "supposedly" because the scores of different publishers' tests and editions of different tests were being compared—a process that is statistically invalid. More important, standardized tests could not measure the remarkable growth that children in developmentally appropriate classrooms make (see Meyer et al., 1998). The newspaper blamed the falling scores on the lack of phonics instruction in the schools.

The reading administrator for the district worked with other district office administrators and a rapidly selected and small group of teachers to quickly choose a phonics program to be used by all primary teachers the following school year. There would be no debate about the use of the program. There would be no year of piloting the programs in a few schools to ensure its quality—a process that was traditional in all previous curriculum adoptions. All primary level teachers were expected to use the program, as scripted, with every child. The adoption caused much strife in the district because some teachers did not see the need for a program that demanded the inclusion of every primary student. In private, some teachers expressed anger and concern at the district's disregard of teacher professionalism.

That didn't matter. The mandate was issued, and principals pretty much demanded that teachers follow the scripted lessons. Some principals required 1 year of participation that would be followed by discussions of the efficacy of the program. Others left subsequent years up in the air. All pretty much demanded adherence to the mandate.

Karen and other teachers felt they were receiving mixed messages from the district office. First, they were told to learn about developmentally appropriate practice; now they are told to follow a mandate that demanded that they disregard their knowledge of the individual needs of their students. The phonics mandate had more clout and was what teachers were expected to follow. Teachers like Karen invited me into their classrooms to verify their understanding of what they were seeing during the teaching of phonics. They invited me for support because of the self-doubt they began to feel as the climate in the district shifted toward a lack of trust in teachers' knowledge of and effectiveness in the teaching and learning of reading.

This is not meant to portray teachers as weak and helpless or me as someone who could remedy the situation. I was also seeking support and validation as colleagues began ordering phonics programs to use with preservice teachers and the state was putting pressure on universities to prepare teachers to teach phonics as the main focus of beginning reading programs.

Although teachers talked to each other about the mandate, they also began feeling isolated and sometimes weary. They wanted confirmation. They wanted someone to substantiate for them that the program was doing what they saw it doing. They were concerned about the pressure put on them to use the mandated program and the district's unwillingness to listen to teachers' concerns about its impact on children and teachers. They wanted another pair of eyes to see, respond, empathize, and validate their interpretations of lessons such as the one described in chapter 2. Confident teachers were doubting themselves while feeling angry and incredulous of their own observations of their classrooms. For some, their confidence was a recent development, cultivated when the climate of the district was supportive of professional teachers making decisions. Now they just couldn't believe what they were being forced to do.

Before going much further, it is important to note that the district is not the villain in this story. The district responded to intense and unrelenting public pressure. Editorials by parents and taxpayers put pressure on the district office. There were national pressures, discussed in later chapters, that also painted pictures of a severe national reading problem that must be dealt with immediately and in one very particular way—through the use of systematic intense direct instruction phonics programs. The national efforts showed themselves locally, using strategies that embarrassed the district. The district followed other districts and made the decision to appease the local outcry by adopting a phonics program.

MY ROLE AND AN INVISIBLE TEACHER

In my past writings (Meyer, 1996; Meyer et al., 1998), I included teachers' voices, their names, and teachers' and students' accomplishments. In this book, however, "Karen" is a pseudonym. Her identity remains hidden because teachers throughout the district began to feel vulnerable as they were silenced at staff and district meetings. Their questions or challenges about the mandate were dismissed or responded to with such severity that it became clear that they had to acquiesce (or feign acquiescence) to the mandate. Their vulnerability included fear of reprimand for disagreeing with the district mandate and even fear of losing their jobs.

There is for me, then, an element of fear in my writing of this book— fear that I make public here to acknowledge the severity and intensity of the effects of mandates such as the one to use a single phonics program for every child. My fear is that by my exposing of a poor choice that a district has made, a teacher is vulnerable. I do not want a teacher to be vulnerable for cooperating with me in a research study. So I have made Karen invisible. To honor Karen's understanding that she might be punished, she must remain invisible. Sometimes it may sound as if I am talking for her, but I am not. I believe that I am advocating for her. I try to portray her as thoughtful and caring as she is, but not with enough detail that she can ever be identified. I present some of her words and many of her understandings of the effects of the program.

So Karen remains hidden and somewhat silenced.

I, however, do not.

I was engaged in various research projects in the district. As I said, this involved study groups and presentations. After the phonics mandate, as schools shifted in the nature of their activity, I continued studying and learning in classrooms. I kept collecting field notes. I kept analyzing the field notes. In classroom after classroom, teachers I know and love shifted their practices to fit the district mandate. I watched as student teachers (whom I taught in methods courses before their student teaching and sometimes observed during their student teaching so that I could write them letters of recommendation) taught phonics lessons. I heard many complaints and questions about the phonics program. The program and teachers' responses to it began to saturate the data I was collecting in classrooms. I had a huge amount of data on literacy activity and the way it was changing in the district when Karen asked me to visit her classroom, a classroom I had visited before.

THE PHONICS EXPERIENCE UP-CLOSE
AND PERSONAL

The classroom visits I was making were haunting me because of the changes teachers were making and their comments about these changes being forced on them. I studied and analyzed the data and then returned to my notes of my visit to Karen's classroom. Being a researcher who relies on anthropological methods for my research (Glaser & Strauss, 1967; Spradley, 1980), I had copious notes with an abundance of the children's and teacher's exact words. I thought of all the research about phonics I'd read and listened to at professional conferences. The important and nagging missing element in much of that research is that nowhere in the research do we get to see what life is like during phonics instruction. The intimate view presented in this book opens the door to interpreting phonics programs from multiple perspectives that are based on the lived experience of children and their teachers.

I could find research reports of classrooms in which phonics was incorporated as part of much larger literacy pictures (Mills, O'Keeffe, & Stephens, 1992). There are also wonderful books written by teacher-researchers about lives in classrooms (Atwell, 1998; Avery, 1993; Fisher, 1998; Fraser & Skolnick, 1996; Hindley, 1996). These offer descriptions of a full school year, including the setting up of the physical space and the activities that transpire each day. These books are powerful reads and required reading in beginning literacy courses that I teach. However, the books do not focus on what happens in the classroom when a systematic, direct, intense phonics program is required by the district. No one listened closely to a teacher to portray her lived experiences. No one observed children closely during phonics lessons to see the ways in which the lessons affected them.

I realized that there needs to be a place for others to see, think about, and work to understand not only that phonics involves the teaching of the sounds that letters make, but that such instruction is significant on other levels. We need to understand what such instruction suggests about the definition of what readers are, what reading is, and what readers should ultimately be able to do. We need to understand the lessons about teaching, learning, language, and more that children are receiving when they are taught phonics through a mandated program. We need to understand at the level of what is happening for the definition of what it means to be a teacher. We need to understand the impact of such programs on what curriculum is, how decisions about curriculum are made, and how such decision making influences the lives of children in classrooms. Whoa! Too much of a leap, you might think.

Yes, this might seem like quite a leap, particularly if you believe that you are simply trying to teach reading. Maybe you have some struggling readers in your classroom or your home and you merely want to have the struggling readers say the sounds that go with the letters on the page so that they are reading. It's that simple, isn't it? Some teachers and researchers may argue that it is that simple. They tell stories of teaching a struggling reader to read by intensively focusing on the relationships between what is written on the page and the sounds that a reader is supposed to make. Well, if it's that simple, why does this supposed war rage on?

IT'S NOT THAT SIMPLE

Sorry. It's not that simple. (Don't you just hate when a writer says that?) But it's not merely "not that simple" so that I get to write a book on phonics. Reading and learning to read are not that simple because of the complexity of the human mind and because of the ways in which we learn as we experience something (Wells, 1999). Rather than offer readers a long treatise on such intellectually lofty topics as the tension between experiences and knowledge construction, let's look at a situation in a real classroom.

That's why I wrote this book: so that we can get an intimate view of the phonics experience in a primary level classroom. I want to give the view from the perspective of lived classroom experience; that is, I want to present an in-depth description so that you might be able to see one representative phonics experience like a movie in your mind. From that view, I offer ways to interpret what happened during the teaching of phonics. Yes, it gets a little complicated, but in intriguing ways that may help us understand how to make choices that ensure success for young readers. After all, isn't that success what we're supposed to be about?

REALLY? JUST ONE LESSON?

In the following chapter, I introduce Karen and her classroom quite briefly. Then we get a close look at a phonics lesson. The lesson is typical of those that she delivers each day of the school year until she completes the number of lessons required at her grade level. She might finish those by March. Each day is the same; the content might shift slightly, but each day the lesson follows a pattern and uses activities that become quite familiar to the children. As you will see, they've quickly learned what their roles in the lessons are and they assume those roles with an eerie ease. There are rarely surprises, although on this day there is one surprise as Karen introduces something not in the script because the lesson takes so long.

The presentation of one lesson is meant to be emblematic; by that I mean that the one lesson signifies or stands for what it is that Karen does daily in her classroom. She is quick to admit that, "If you've seen one of these lessons, you've seen them all," except that the particular letter or sound being studied varies. Although it may appear to make sense that we teach the little pieces of language to children this way, ultimately such instruction may be accomplishing the opposite of what we want for our children as readers, for their schools as places to learn, and for the citizens we want them to become.

The idea of using a "thick description" (Geertz, 1973) of an actual classroom event to represent many such events and gain insights into the lives of learners (including teachers) in those events is not new. Over 100 years ago, Herbart (1895) explained that:

> Never . . . can [science] be a substitute for observation of the pupil; the individual can only be discovered, not deduced. The construction of the pupil on *a priori* principles is therefore a misleading expression in itself, and is also at present an empty idea which the science of education cannot handle for a long time. (p. 78)

In other words, if we think (or show through various statistical means) that *something* is working for students learning to read, we owe it to the students whose lives are influenced by that *something* to look closely at **how** it is working in classrooms.

If you are interested in other references about the validity of presenting one scenario and using it as a basis for a book, you might consult Guba and Lincoln (1982), who reminded us "that the general resides in the particular and . . . what one learns from a particular [situation] applies to other situations subsequently encountered" (p. 7). Wolcott (1990) suggested that when we write thick descriptions, we should not dismiss validity, but "attempt to put it into some broader perspective" (p. 148). The broader perspective in this book is that discussions of the validity of mandated phonics programs must include the ways in which such programs influence literacy, teaching, learning, and life within and beyond the classroom. My hope is that readers can use the thinking I've done in this book as a mirror on practices they are asked to enact or support in classrooms.

With all that I've written in this chapter as the background (the context) of Karen's teaching of phonics, let's look at Karen and her students during a phonics lesson.

2

Phonics Lessons

If you've seen one of these lessons, you've seen them all.
—Karen, a primary grade teacher

THE CONTEXT

Karen teaches a primary level grade in a medium-size city. When I read about teachers and students at various schools, I typically expect the description to include the socioeconomic status (SES) and ethnic and cultural makeup of the student body. I am not including those data here for reasons discussed in greater depth in chapter 7. As you read the description that follows, make some guesses about how the authors of the phonics program view the relevance of SES, ethnicity, and culture in the teaching they prescribe.

Karen was in a study group with some of her colleagues, and so were other teachers in her district as it moved toward developmentally appropriate practice. She was in a master's program and took courses from me, as did other teachers. She went to conferences locally, at the state level, and nationally, as did other teachers in the district. Teachers were supported in attending the International Reading Association, Whole Language Umbrella, National Council of Teachers of English, National Council of Teachers of Mathematics, National Council of Teachers of Social Studies, Multiage Conferences, Multiple Intelligence conferences, and more. The district had a history of supporting teachers as learners. Karen is a learner. That's about all I can tell you about her without increasing my fear of her being identified

As I said in chapter 1, the district's second-grade reading scores were published in the local newspaper. The interpretation offered to the public was that **the** scores (implying all the scores of children across all grade levels) had gone down in all but one school although only second-grade scores were published. The dismal picture of second-grade readers—extended to all students in the district—was presented, argued over in editorials and on local radio talk shows, and precipitated the adoption of one phonics program for all primary students.

Both at district inservice sessions and via directives from principals, every kindergarten, first-, second-, and third-grade teacher was instructed to follow the manuals verbatim during the first year of implementation. Like many other teachers in the district, Karen met with her principal to question the mandate. She was frustrated that some of her students' needs were not addressed by the program, but was told to use the program as scripted for one year.

THE INVITATION

Early in the new school year, many primary teachers were disenchanted with the program. In graduate courses, when I ran into them in supermarkets, and through student teachers, they relayed messages to me of their dissatisfaction. It was in this milieu that I once again met Karen; I was participating in a district inservice day she attended.

"Rick," she began on seeing me, "You would not recognize my teaching this year." I'd visited her classroom in previous years and was always drawn into the discussions of reading and writing in which she engaged her young students.

"I'm hearing that a lot this year," I answered.

"You would not believe what we have to do," she sighed.

"I'm so sorry." I didn't know what else to say.

"You've got to come and see this."

"I will," I responded.

We agreed that I would observe her teaching one morning in the coming week. The following description is elaborated from the notes I took during that visit.

IT'S TIME FOR PHONICS

I arrive at Karen's classroom as the children are completing their morning opening activities with the student teacher in charge. The date has been discussed and entered onto the calendar, and the news from one child is written on large chart paper. The class rereads the news together, and the student teacher, having completed her portion of the morning activities, looks at Karen. Karen tells the children it is time for phonics. Karen's use of words is significant and intentional: "I will not call *that* reading," she told me earlier. "It's not reading."

It is a little before 10:00. The time is important because you'll get a sense of how long it took to complete phonics on the day I visited. Here, then, is a typical phonics lesson. The scripted teachers' guide for the program is further evidence of the routine. Subsequent visits to Karen's classroom and to others around the district further confirm the routine of the phonics program in primary classrooms. As Karen said, it is always the same.

STARTING THE LESSON

The children are seated on the carpeted floor in no particular arrangement; they are facing Karen, who sits in a chair in front of a white markerboard that is fixed to the wall (the way that chalkboards were once at the front of classrooms). Typical of Karen's classrooms as I'd seen them in the past, the walls have student work on them, it is light and cheery, and the children's desks are arranged into tables of three to six children.

Karen begins the lesson by telling the children that they will do a "you blend them story." She reads from the scripted guide in front of her that tells the group of 18 children—10 girls and 8 boys—to pay attention as she begins to read the old fable of the crow and the fox. You know the story: The fox wants the cheese that the very vain crow has in its beak. The fox tells the crow that she can't sing that well; when the crow sings to convince the fox that she can sing, she drops the cheese and the fox eats it. This story typically lends itself to discussions of gender, beauty, chicanery, and more as readers or listeners transact (Rosenblatt, 1978) with it.

However, in this classroom, on this day, the scenario is different because this is a "you blend them story." Karen begins telling the story. In the following, when I put letters in //, it indicates the sounds for which those letters stand. When the letters are in < >, it means the name of the letter. When I refer to words that Karen writes on the board, they are underlined.

Karen begins to read: "Once there was a /k/-/r/-/o/ [she is making the sounds that, blended together, say the word *crow*]."

Some children call out, "Crow!" Others follow suit, saying, "crow" as well, just a beat after the first bunch. The second group is taking its cues from the children who understand the task.

As Karen continues through the story, she stops at every fifth word or so and says the sounds (phonemes) that make up the word. She is reading from a scripted lesson that tells her what to say. The children cannot see the words of the story; they are only listening. Karen haltingly says the individual sounds to make these words: /f/-/o/-/x/, /l/-/u/-/n/-/ch/, /sh/-/i/-/n/ [shine], /v/-/oi/-/s/ [voice], /b/-/ea/-/k/, and /n/-/u/-/n/ [none], following the script that demands that she stretch these particular words into their separate phonemes. After the story, there is a brief discussion, but it seemed to me that only the children who said they were familiar with the fable could answer the questions. Karen confirms my suspicion after the lesson, explaining that her stronger readers (and those not frustrated or tuned out) are the ones who typically follow the storyline during this type of activity. Many others, including Karen at times, get lost in the sounds. I, too, had lost the thrust of the story until I stopped to remind myself that I knew it already.

SUBSTITUTING FINAL SOUNDS

By 10:05, the story is completed. Karen turns toward (and asks the children to look at) the markerboard at the front of the room. She writes super-man on the board. Two children call out, "Superman!" right away. I will learn later that they are quite precocious readers that will volunteer many of the words Karen writes. The transition has been wordless as the children watch their teacher shift from reading the scripted story to writing a word on the board. They are used to the routine; it's almost October and they've been at this for many weeks.

Karen erases the <n> on superman and puts a <d> at the end to make the nonword, supermad. Perhaps you will argue that it is a word. Some of the students in Karen's class would agree, and one of the children suggests that if you are very mad at someone, you "are supermad at them." Next Karen puts an <n> back, in place of the <d>, but then places a <d> after the <n> to make supermand. Saying the whole thing very slowly, the children work to call the nonword. One calls it out, and the rest echo what that child has said. They look at their teacher; "What is 'supermand'?" asks one.

Karen says, "It is not a word."

Karen erases supermand and writes baboon; one of the same two precocious readers reads it. Karen changes it to baboot. Some of the children say it; others echo it. Some of the children are silent.

Next, Karen writes alphabet; the same two children read it. Others echo it. Karen changes it to alphabed. Some children chuckle as they read it; others echo the word and wait for the next word. I wonder if they are curious what an alphabed is. Again, about five are silent.

When Karen writes schoolbus, some say it and others echo it. Someone suggests, "Like *The Magic School Bus* [books]" (Cole, 1986), as Karen turns it into schoolbun by erasing the <s> and replacing it with an <n>. One child frowns and calls out, "Ms. L, what is a 'schoolbun'?" One of the children responds before Karen can answer. He says, "Like, when you're at school, if they have hot dogs for lunch, they give it to you on a schoolbun."

The last word that the children will have to read in its original and altered form during this day's lesson is recess. Because this word is used on the daily schedule, more children than the few precocious readers say it. I watch with some of the children as it is changed into reced; Karen erases <ss> and writes <d> at the end. Can you pronounce that word? How would you pronounce it if you hadn't seen "recess" first? Karen pronounces this by saying the prefix "re" with the word *said*. "Here's a challenge: write 'reced' on a piece of paper and ask someone to read it who has not seen 'recess' first. Some will think that you wanted to write 'raced.' Others will make the /k/ sound for the <c>. Still others will say something like 'rest'." This part of the lesson is called phonological or phonemic awareness by Karen when we talk about it. She uses the two (phonological and phonemic) interchangeably when we talk. She explains that it's meant to teach about sounds and words, but she thinks that the nonsensical focus derails that intention. She explains that children want meaning first and that the presentation of nonwords confuses them, especially those just beginning to read. That portion of the lesson is over and Karen shifts to the next portion.

SNIGGLES AND FINAL SOUNDS

It's now 10:08. Karen announces, "Let's get out Sniggle." Sniggle[1] is the hand puppet that the students have named. "Figure out what Sniggle is doing today," Karen says, again reading from the script. Karen promised her principal that she would give the phonics program a fair consideration for

---

[1]The name of this puppet has also been changed as part of my effort to maintain Karen's anonymity.

this school year. Part of honoring that promise is reading the script for each lesson exactly as the publisher intended. She slips her hand inside the puppet to work its mouth.

Karen holds Sniggle facing her; she says, "Maze." Then she moves her hand so that the puppet faces the children, she moves the puppet's lips, and she changes her voice as she says /zzzz/. She says "man" following the same routine, with Sniggle facing her when she says the word and making Sniggle face the children when the puppet says the isolated final sound of the word. Sniggle the puppet says /nnnn/. She says "fish" and the puppet says /shhhh/. Her change in voice and movement of the puppet is intended to cue the children into the activity. The teacher is saying one thing; the puppet is saying something else. The children are to figure out what the puppet is doing and do that along with it.

A child suggests that the puppet is saying the ending sound; Karen confirms this, and the children say the ending sound of these words, along with Sniggle: "sleep," "touch," "leak," "meet," "truck," "treat," "place," "eat," "please," and "teach." Karen is serious about this work. She is enacting the script carefully and conscientiously, yet each time that Sniggle faces her, her eyes cross ever so slightly as she says the cue word to the puppet. I do not insert this information to imply that Karen is acting foolishly. Rather, I mention it because her intensity at enacting the script is figuratively and literally forcing her to lose or sacrifice sight of what she knows about reading, teaching, and learning.

After the lesson, Karen explained how exhausting it is to follow the scripted lessons because her focus has to be on the material to be covered rather than children learning reading. She also tells me that she's concerned that puppets do not get to speak full words, sentences, and more in this program. She does not like demonstrating to her students such an unimaginative use of puppets. I picture confused family members as children go home and play with puppets that make sounds but don't say any words. Karen says "Thank you for helping us" to Sniggle and places him back in his box near her desk.

INTRODUCING <D> AND /D/

At 10:12, Karen asks the student teacher to put the overhead projector in place. The student teacher wheels it to a spot behind all the children and aims it at the markerboard; she plugs it in, but she does not turn it on. Karen holds up a white card that measures about 12 by 18 inches with upper-

and lowercase <d> printed on it. The publisher of the program provides these cards.

She says, "The uppercase <D> is a straight line down from the sky and a big fat tummy. The lowercase <d> is a circle and then a straight line down." She says this twice, drawing the letters in the air with her index finger. Some of the children draw in the air with her.

I look above the markerboard at the front of the room, where one might see the alphabet in a primary classroom. There is a row of white cards the size of the one Karen is holding. Six of them have an upper- and lowercase letter (e.g., <Dd>) and an illustration. One of those cards is the letter <a>; the other five are consonants. The rest of the cards are blank.

Karen turns over the card she is holding to reveal the letters <d> and <D> again; this side of the card also has a picture of a dinosaur. Some of the children seem excited and talk to Karen and each other about dinosaurs.

SCANNING THE SCENE

It's 10:14, and I look around at the group of young children. This is the first of a few "scans" that I do; a scan is a research strategy in which the researcher looks a little more broadly at the context or setting. I had been focusing intensely on Karen's actions and some of the children's responses. A scan is an opportunity to step back and look at the whole group to further capture the nature of the experience.

I notice that some of the children are watching Karen; others are not. One child has carefully rolled up one leg of his jeans and works at unraveling his sock. He is making a little ball with the string of elastic as he unweaves. Because he is unweaving only the threads that are parallel to the sole of his foot, he is leaving a sort of skeleton of his sock that starts to slip down his leg as he unwraps further. A few of the children are rocking back and forth, seemingly not paying particular attention to Karen (although at this point in time it is conjecture to suggest they are not paying attention merely because they are not looking at her). One child is quietly making the sounds of bombs dropping ("eeeeyowwwwwww plichhhh") as he moves his hand above the rug, drops it slowly toward the rug, and makes the sound when his hand hits the rug. He does this repeatedly. One of the children picks his nose; another plays with her ears; one more is rubbing her hands up and down her braids (later she'll undo and redo them).

A STORY WITH LOTS OF <d>S

The student teacher turns on the overhead and focuses it to reveal a story about a dinosaur. The story is about eight lines long and fits on the top half of the overhead. Karen reads it as the student teacher points to each word. The story has a lot of <d>s in it. At the end of every few lines are two-letter <d>s written side by side (<dd>). The children are to say the sound /d/ two times when they come to the parts of the story where <dd> is written. The sound is supposed to represent the sound of dinosaurs walking.

The experience with the story is short, and the children focus back on Karen as the overhead is turned off. It took only 2 minutes to read it. There was no discussion of the storyline. Later Karen will explain that the push to complete the lesson makes discussion impossible—there's just not time for it. She also tells me that it is not called for in the script.

As the children look to Karen for what they are to do next, my eyes focus once again above the markerboard. I notice that the letter <h> is one of the letters that can be seen; the card has a picture of a dog near the letters. I whisper to the child next to me, "What is that picture on the card with <h> and a dog?" I realize that I've answered my own question (it is a dog), but I think she understands that I'm asking about a dog being on the <h> card.

She smiles and says, "That's a /h/ /h/ /h/ hound dog."

I smile back. She has breathed big puffs of air with each /h/, and we both think she's quite clever.

LISTENING FOR /d/ . . . AND CHILDREN'S
RESPONSE PATTERNS

Karen reads from the scripted teachers guide: "Say these words back to me if they start with /d/ /d/." She says the sound of <d> twice. Then she reads: dog, daisy, dance, foot, dark, wagon, doorman, and paper, and the list goes on for about 12 words. She pauses after saying each word and waits for children to repeat the words that begin with <d>. The pattern of children responding at this point in the lesson is consistent with what has occurred earlier in the lesson. A small number of children respond almost in unison. Some of the children wait for those initial responses and then mimic them. Some of the children say every word regardless of the initial consonant sound. Still others are silent for the entire activity.

Throughout this lesson (and the others I have seen like it), children's responses fit into categories. The first category is the "we get it gang." These are the children who understand the demands of the activity and respond with the answer demanded by the script; in this activity, they call back words that have an initial /d/. My guess is that most of these children already know what the lesson is teaching. Karen later tells me that most of the children that quickly volunteer responses are, indeed, those who are already proficient readers and writers.

The second category of student response comes from my understanding of David Bloome's (1983) work in classrooms. He found that students often act to perpetuate an activity in school, even though they may not understand the activity. He referred to this type of student behavior as *procedural display*. In other words, these students may not understand the content of what is being presented to them, but they understand what school is supposed to look like and work to sustain the process of the lesson. This group of students has learned that in the phonics lessons the teacher talks and the students respond by saying a sound or a word aloud. I call this second category of response "procedural display participation." In the initial /d/ activity, the students in the procedural display participation category call back only those words with an initial /d/, but do so only after waiting for and echoing the "we get it gang's" response (or lack of response if there is no /d/ at the beginning of the word Karen calls). These children are echoing the correct response; they've learned how to respond by identifying children successful at the task and following them. My guess is that many of them are more focused on their colleagues' responses during the lesson than on learning the sound of the letter <d>.

This second category, procedural display participation, is interesting because during the lesson there is no way of telling whether the children in this category are learning or already know the material. At this point, it is their vicarious participation that is interesting because of its ambiguity; we just don't know what's going on in their minds.

The third category is "random responses." These occur as some children call back either random words or every word regardless of the word Karen calls. Some children in this category remained silent for much of the lesson. It is difficult to tell what children in this category are learning.

A DIVERSION

At 10:19, Karen says, "You all seem very restless because of all this phonics." It is here that something quite remarkable occurs. I expect she will tell them that they'll go outside for a break. I'm a seasoned teacher, having taught young children for almost 20 years, and quietly rejoice in the opportunity to stretch my legs. Earlier, I noted some behaviors that might suggest that the children needed a break of some sort as well. However, Karen's response to the restlessness is one I do not expect. She says, "I've got a real book about dinosaurs here." She holds up a large picture book that has a big dinosaur on the cover. The scripted lesson has been placed aside. As Karen reads and shows them the pictures, the frustration behaviors that I noted abate. The sock unweaver, who is one of the precocious readers, moves closer to Karen and looks at the book as she reads. Other children also move closer to the book. The nose picker stops. The rocking that some of the children were engaged in also stops during the reading of the story. The child who played with his ears and the kids who were chatting with their friends instead of watching Sniggle or echoing nonwords are now focused. As she reads, Karen is emotional and active and changes her voice for different characters. The children interrupt the reading at times for brief comments and thoughts connected to the story.

It's 10:33. They discuss the story, including the genre. For the next few minutes, the children make connections to other texts they've read and talk about what they know and wonder about dinosaurs. The talk about the book winds down, and Karen excuses the children to write in their journals for 15 minutes. She tells them that phonics is not done and that they'll have to return to finish today's lesson. She tells them that she wants them to "enjoy writing for a while" before they continue. The children chat as they return to their desks, find their journals, and write. Some of them share their writing with each other and with Karen. Twenty minutes after they were excused, she calls them back to the markerboard area. "Let's finish phonics," Karen says.

BACK TO THE SCRIPT AND A SECOND SCAN

It's almost 10:55. The children are seated on the rug again. They are asked to say these words as Karen writes them on the markerboard. She writes dad and changes it to had to mad; she writes an and changes it to and to hand; she writes ant and changes it to can to cat to can to can't. Some of the children watched as Karen wrote the words and erased parts to make new words. Others did not. Once again, I scan the group of children sitting closely together on the rug. I see: a child picking her nose and examining the findings; one child poking (in a friendly manner) another; one pulling at the rug; the sock child is, once again, tearing apart his clothing; one child talks to a friend; one sits and rocks and twists his ears; one unbraids and braids her hair; one sucks his bracelet; one is squatting, rather than sitting on her bottom; one is rolling; and one is styling her cuticles with her thumbnail. Without looking up, some answer mechanically, some echo, and others ignore as Karen asks them to say what she wrote.

This behavior stands in stark contrast to what I observed during the journal writing time that the children just completed. During that time, children read and reread what they wrote. They read their writing to others near them and asked for advice. They read to Karen and to me. They moved around the room to find words they wanted to spell or to write near a friend. They asked questions of each other of their writing. A few who did not seem interested in journal writing listened for a while, watched their colleagues, and then—as if an idea struck—began writing, too. The one child who appeared to be staring at the ceiling and couldn't think of anything to write interested me. When I asked him about journal writing, he explained that some days he just daydreams. He also showed me his journal, which was thick with stories, illustrations, and events from his life.

LETTERS ON CARDS

Once again, Karen moves from one scripted activity to the next. At 11:10, she has the children pick up letter cards with <m>, <n>, <c>, <d>, and <a> on them. These are some of the same letters that are displayed above the markerboard at the front of the room. The <a> is printed in red, and the rest are black. On one side, the cards look like a conventional deck of playing cards; one letter is on the other side of each card. They pick up the cards from piles on a nearby table, and they form a large circle upon returning to the rug area. Karen has not asked that the circle be formed. The children know this routine and immediately start to make words and call them out. Being in a circle allows them to see each other's cards.

Some make "mad," and Karen asks them to say the sounds of each letter in "mad." Others look at their colleagues who have formed the word successfully by putting the cards with <m>, <a>, and <d> together and find those letters to make the word themselves. Others finger the cards and move them around, not paying particular attention to the word Karen acknowledges and asks them all to make. One child calls out "dam" and is accused of making a bad word, but Karen clarifies that this is a thing that holds water back, not the bad word. One says he could make "candy" if he had a <y>. Karen says, "That is harder than we're supposed to make." This is the only time in the lesson that she looks over the children at me. Her eyes fill with water. In just a few minutes, the children make words suggested by their colleagues or the publishers (via Karen). The cards are collected.

Later, when I ask Karen about her feelings when she responded to that child, she explains that the program underestimates some children and confuses others. "It's just not for every child," she sighs.

A BOOK, OF SORTS

The closing part of the lesson, beginning at almost 11:20, involves the distribution of a "book" made from a blackline master. The book fits onto one piece of photocopy paper, with each page being one half of the piece of paper. When the book is folded, it will have four pages. The book is illustrated with simple line drawings. It is about a cat that naps on a mat, on a (mouse) pad, in a pan, and in a cap. The cat's owner is illustrated as being annoyed at the cat's choices of places to nap. The only words in the book are: "the," "cat," "had," "nap," "on," "a," "mat," "pad," "in," "pan," and "cap." Some of the words are used in one sentence on each page of the book. The children read the text in a mass oral reading; more accurately, some read, some echo, some ignore. This is followed by a flurry of rereading to a few neighbors. They briefly discuss the naughty cat in the book. Karen says they may color it later on. The children's immediate reading of the book, en masse, suggests how familiar they are with the routine of the lessons. They know when they are to read and reread.

After they read the book a few times to each other, one child leans back to a nearby bookshelf and grabs a stapler. He places the single folded sheet of paper (referred to by the scripted lesson as a book) into the stapler and staples it so that it looked like the books they sometimes made during their now-infrequent writers workshop. But the books the children make during writers workshop have many more sheets of paper in them. The children are accustomed to writing longer books than the one they just read; those longer books are held together with staples. There really was no need for staples as far as I could tell. However, looking closely on the sheet that a child near me had, I could see two half-inch lines right at the fold of the paper, suggesting the placement of a staple over each one. The stapler is passed around the circle and all of the children staple their books.

Karen asks the children to put their books into their book bags, square plastic bags (12 inches by 12 inches) that seal at the top. The children keep these in their desks so that they have books handy if there's time for reading. Some of the children have been reading rather complex texts, such as *The Magic School Bus* (Cole, 1986); others have more predictable (not just phonetically regular) books like *Brown Bear, Brown Bear* (Martin, 1983) in their bags. The program provided other books like the one about the cat, and some of the children have those in their bags. Karen has a book of blackline masters (photocopy quality sheets for reproduction and distribution to the students) filled with many more one-page ready-to-fold books to copy for the children during the year.

Each day, Karen is required to do one lesson of this direct instruction, systematic, intense phonics program. When the children are dismissed for lunch, Karen tells me that when she told a district reading administrator that phonics was taking up to 90 minutes on some days, she was told that she has a "personal problem." She makes little quote signs in the air when she says *personal problem*. "What does that mean?" she asks looking at me.

"I don't know." I tell her because I have no idea.

The total time spent on phonics, subtracting the minutes that the children heard a real book and wrote in their journals, was 60 minutes.

LIFE BEFORE THE MANDATE

Life in Karen's classroom before the mandate was different. She says that it was "a more joyous classroom" when Karen felt she was in charge of the time she spent teaching and her students spent learning. Readers and writers workshops were (prior to the mandate) essential parts of the school day. Now they have to be chiseled to a bare minimum and are not part of the school day on some days because phonics comes first. She tells me that she would not "give them" literature, so she works to find time to read books (like the dinosaur text from the library) to her children.

She has, however, "given them" writing. "Them" is a reference to administrators who have changed the use of time in her classroom. "Giving" means that there's just no time left in the day for writers workshop so it is often given up. Given up to the program. Given up to the publishers. Karen explains that she is losing more than the beautiful writing that her children did. By losing writers workshop, she loses insights into what her children know. When they wrote each day, every piece of writing she saw was evidence of what children knew, were coming to know, and might benefit from learning more about. When her students had time to write, she learned what she needed to teach them. In subsequent writing that they did, she could tell if she needed to reteach things or if the children had learned and were applying what she taught.

When there was more time for reading, Karen got much more information about individual students. Using assessment tools such as miscue analysis (Y. Goodman, Watson, & Burke, 1987), she learned what they knew and made decisions about what to teach next. Karen said that she will not "give *them*" her reading program so she doesn't teach science or social studies to have as much time as possible for reading (although not as much as in the past). Still, there is often less time for conversations (Peterson & Eeds, 1990) about books. There is less time for discussions about language. There is less time to ask children, "What do you notice about . . . ?" This was a question Karen used to ask a lot more than she does now. For example, when the month changed, she'd ask what children noticed about the name of the new month. In a few minutes, she'd get information about what children know about initial consonants, final consonants, syllables, alphabetical order, and more. There's just not as much time to ask, "What do you notice?"

When Karen's children have the opportunity to read or listen to longer texts (not short pieces like the abbreviated *Fox and Crow* story or the half-page *Dinosaur* piece from the phonics program), they engage in exciting discussions that feed readers' minds. She is adamant about keeping this time in her day. She says, "My students need to hear stories. They need to be involved with real literature." She can't let go of this, "although I always feel like I'm battling the clock."

When I asked Karen how she taught phonics before the mandate, she smiled. "I taught it all day!" she said. She taught it when the days changed, the months changed, during writing, during reading, during science, math, and social studies. "We always talked about letters, sounds, rhymes, and more." She asked her students how they might spell words and what possibilities there were for letter–sound relationships. She is convinced that in previous years her students took more risks as writers and readers because the pressure on exactness was not there. They always moved toward conventional reading and writing, but did so in a way that did not limit or intimidate writers by insistence on always being correct. She believes that the mandated program is so oriented to preciseness that her students were not willing to take risks as readers and writers. That, in combination with less time for writing, made Karen wonder about all the possibilities that were lost: possibilities for teaching, possibilities for learning, and possibilities for great young writers to express themselves, their ideas, their hopes, their dreams, and their imaginations.

Karen's students lost more than the hour of instructional time to the mandate. They lost some of the energy, vitality, and spirit of their teacher. They lost time to explore ideas by talking, had less time to visit the media center (school library), and had less time to seek sources outside of the classroom (by writing letters, making phone calls, and searching the Internet) that could help address young children's natural curiosity about their worlds (Duckworth, 1987). Karen felt her students "have less time to think like real readers and writers." Their teacher lost access to their minds because the scripted hour severely limited the repertoire of responses they could offer their teacher. These losses, expressed by Karen, are what she mourns.

YOUR THOUGHTS

In what other ways does 1 hour of classroom time spent this way influence the children and the teacher? What were the objectives of the phonics lesson? Who was served? How? How do you know? How were students' previous experiences, their languages, and their cultures brought into the lesson? What else does the lesson suggest? My interpretations of these questions and others are presented in the chapters that follow.

3

What Is Reading?

A word is dead when it is said,
Some say.
I say it just begins to live
That day.

—Emily Dickinson (1951)

DEFINITIONS OF READING

In this chapter, I encourage you to write your definition of reading, I present my definition of reading, I present Karen's definition of reading, and I discuss the definitions offered by other researchers. Then I suggest some ways in which learning phonics in Karen's classroom contributes to her students' definitions of reading and writing. The definition of phonics in the program Karen is using is discussed late in this chapter, but I hope you'll think about that definition as you reflect on chapter 2 and as you read what follows.

Emily Dickinson's poem nags at some of the tension over just what reading is. Has a child in Karen's class read when she says "reced"? Do we consider a child a reader if he looks at the child next to him, organizes some cards the way that child has them, and then says "Mad" because that is what his neighbor says? Has a child *read* if he or she echoes others in a large group of children, all required to read the same word, when the child could not say the word unassisted and does not look at the word while saying it? In other words, is the goal that the child say the word and move on even if that word is a nonword, like "schoolbun," according to an unabridged dictionary. If a child is not engaged beyond this sort of calling out, is the child reading?

The underlying question here is, **"What is reading?"** There is no simple answer. Knowing that there are different definitions enables us to look for the definitions of others in the programs they publish or the policies and curriculum they mandate. Understanding our own definition, and how it is alike or different from those of others, will help us respond to policies and mandates that we find informed or objectionable.

YOUR DEFINITION OF READING

Write your definition of reading. Really do it. Turn to the inside cover of this book or a sheet of scrap paper, or where ever else you decide so that you will have a record of your definition of reading. Also write about where this definition came from, which people in your life and what experiences influenced it, and how it changed depending on where you work and what you are doing. As you read this book, decide whether that definition is something you want to keep or change. Keep your definition handy so that you may refer to it as you read and consider what follows.

MY DEFINITION OF READING

My definition of reading is rooted in Emily Dickinson's poem. My definition of reading is this: Reading is what happens when written words begin to live in the mind, heart, relationships, spirit, and world of someone engaging with text. Reading is about having "the disposition to engage appropriately with texts of different types in order to empower action, thinking, and feeling in the context of purposeful social activity" (Wells & Chang-Wells, 1992, p. 147). Maybe you're wondering, "What about a first grader who doesn't know how to read? Are you going to use that same definition?"

Yes, I am. Because for many years we (myself included) have watched words die as children read them. Am I being a bit too romantic about the whole thing here? I don't think so. In *Stories from the Heart* (1996), I worked to understand and tell the story of my own literacy development and then to help students, teachers, and myself understand our literacy lives. A strong message in the book arose as I recounted a literacy life that included my copying of the dust jackets of books to complete book reports without reading books. I'd learned to get by, to say the word, even to write the word, but those words died on the page and in the air. They never made it to my mind, my heart, my spirit, my relationships, and to the essence of my identity—who I was and who I was becoming. Too many of us have lived books this way in school, and it influences our decisions about teaching and learning. It influences our definition of what reading is, and that definition doesn't change unless we make it change.

My definition of reading has been most influenced by my many years as a teacher and a reader and by researchers who do research in real classrooms with real children. I know that some researchers may need to isolate little bits of language and study them for various reasons, but I cannot subscribe to definitions of reading that are constructed far from actual readers who are learning to read. I also need to base my definition on research that is completed using real texts with those real readers. Studying readers as they read nonwords might be informative to some theories of what reading is, but those theories must be verified in real texts with real readers. K. Goodman (1996) put it this way:

> Reductionist research in reading has inevitably focussed on recognition of bits and pieces of language rather than on comprehension of real texts. But we can't assume that perception of letters and words in the process of making sense of real meaningful texts is the same as recognizing letters and words in isolation or in highly reduced contexts. And we can't assume that comprehension follows successive recognition of words. (p. 5)

Goodman's thoughts demand some hard questioning of definitions of reading. He is asking why we should assume that if children read little bits of language they would transfer that to other things they read. He is asking whether the calling aloud of the sounds of letters and real and nonwords means that a child is reading.

Hold my definition of reading up to yours. How do they compare?

KAREN'S DEFINITION OF READING

Karen cultivated her definition of reading as she became increasingly informed about the reading process. She took courses about reading and studied her own and her students' literacy lives in an effort to change what reading was in her own life and in the lives of her students. Karen asserts that a teacher cannot "separate teaching reading from reading. Children need to read like real readers and write like real writers from the beginning of school." She said that real readers do study words and sounds that letters make within words. They consider sounds and letters more closely "when things stop making sense in what they are reading." Her definition is a lot like Goodman's in that she teaches readers that reading is about making meaning.

When Karen looked over the heads of the children with tears in her eyes, it was because she knew what she was doing. She knew that for an hour each day she set aside her definition of reading and yielded to the district's definition. This was painful for her because her definition was one that she constructed by being a thoughtful professional who is informed about reading. She understands that a classroom is a potential for children's literate lives, and it is a potential that she has worked, in past years, to realize and help children realize. The setting aside of her professional knowledge causes pain; it makes her cry.

WHAT IS A DEFINITION OF READING FOR?

A definition of reading cannot stand alone; it must be attached to an explanation of what reading is for—how we read and why. Even young children, such as Karen's primary level students, are learning what reading is for as they learn to read, learn through reading, and learn about reading (Halliday, 1988) via experiences they are having within and beyond the classroom. What I like about the definition I presented at the beginning of this chapter is that it tells what I (along with Wells & Chang-Wells) understand reading to be *for*. Reading is for the beginning and sustaining of bringing life to our relationships with texts.

A definition is more than something that is written in a dictionary. Once a teacher or researcher has developed or arrived at a definition of reading, then that teacher's or researcher's (or politician's or anyone else's) definition is the point of origin for things such as: the way to teach reading, expectations of readers, programs to use or endorse, and research to be carried out. A definition of reading leads to policy decisions that affect children and teachers' lives in schools.

SOME DEFINITIONS OF READING

The whole idea of reading as meaning-based is at the heart of my definition, as it is of this one (which I found in Weaver, 1994):

Reading is the active process of reconstructing meaning from language represented by graphic symbols (letters), just as listening is the active process of reconstructing meaning from the sound symbols (phonemes) of oral language. (Smith, Goodman, & Meredith, 1970, p. 247)

Even as we strive to have more neurologically and physiologically informed definitions of reading, we cannot neglect the human mind. All healthy humans are born with wonderful **brains**. It is not until we begin learning (which might even happen before birth) that our **minds** become involved. This is an important distinction. Our brains are the physical, chemical, and electrical biological stuff that lies within our skulls. Our minds use our lived experiences, our vicarious experiences, our ever-emerging identities, and more to make meaning. The relationship between brain and mind in reading can be explained this way:

When the light rays from the printed page hit the retinal cells of the eyes, signals are sent along the optic nerve to the visual centers of the *brain*. This is not reading. The *mind* must function in the process, the signals must be interpreted, and the reader must give significance to what he [or she] reads. [Readers] must bring *meaning* to the graphic symbol. (Dechant, 1970, p. 12; cited in Weaver, 1994, emphasis added)

Meaning, at the heart of all experiences, is at the heart of reading. In Karen's class, the kids searched for and volunteered meaning when it was hard to find. Rather urgently, they constructed definitions for nonwords, and that constructing demonstrates their commitment to having this *stuff* called "words" make sense. As the children experienced the hour of phonics, the publishers of the program affected the children's definitions of reading. Any experience with written language is an experience that teaches about: the language; the teacher; the rules for learning; and the place, role, and nature of written text in the classroom and the world. These experiences contribute to and influence the reader's definition of reading, which goes to the heart of the individual, to their literacy identity (Martens, Flurkey, Meyer, & Udell, 1999). The relationships among reading, identity, and experience may be summarized this way:

The reader brings to the text his [or her] past experience and present personality. Under the magnetism of the ordered symbols of the text, he [or she] marshals his [or her] resources and crystallizes out from the stuff of memory, thought, and feeling a new order, a new experience, which he [or she] sees as the poem [not necessarily what we think of as a poem, but *any* literary work created by a reader in the process of reading a text]. This becomes part of the ongoing stream of his [or her] life experience, to be reflected on from any angle important to him [or her] as a human being. (Rosenblatt, 1978, p. 12)

A child's definition of reading is shaped by the child's experiences. When a teacher can honor developing definitions based in meaning and meaning-making, the child's understanding of what reading is and what it is for is consistent with Rosentblatt's. My concern is the definition of reading that children are developing when a full hour of their school day, every school day, is devoted to activities that are not based in meaning. Their developing definitions of reading will contain the notion that reading is the calling of sounds to gain a "right answer," rather than meaning. Furthermore, if meaning is not at the root of all instruction, I can't think of reasons that children would want to read. My fear is that by having meaning divorced from reading, children will learn that reading is words being put to death.

RESEARCHERS DON'T AGREE
ON WHAT READING IS

In the prior discussion, I presented some ideas of what reading is and suggested that you write your definition. I also presented some researchers' definitions of reading. Quite often, we hear someone say, "Well, the research says . . ." and then some supposed authority tells us something about reading. Yet researchers do not agree on what reading is. Next, I present some of what researchers write as their definitions of reading. To be honest, sometimes when I read a book like this, I skip the stuff that is in smaller writing, which is typically quotes by other authors. Well, DON'T DO IT! I searched all over to find these! They're here so you can compare and contrast them to what you believe reading to be. They're also here to inform you about how I will interpret and explain what reading is in Karen's classroom.

Weaver (1994) collated some definitions of reading from various reading researchers. I'll interject some of my own comments about some of the definitions to raise questions or issues inherent in some of them. Here's Flesch's (1955) definition of reading:

Reading means getting meaning from certain combinations of letters. Teach the child what each letter stands for and he can read. (p. 17)

Is the researcher making a leap between getting meaning and the sounds of letters? Do you think that if children learn the sounds of letters they can get meaning? Here are some letters put together in a way that you can probably say, but you decide if you are *reading:*

She flumped the garzatious zimper when the flittle wouldn't grantinate.

Well is that reading? Is it reading if you can answer questions about the sentence? I bet you can answer these questions. I bet you can answer them in full sentences!

1. What did she do?
2. What kind of zimper was it?
3. What would not grantinate?
4. When did she flump?

Need help? I doubt it, but here are my answers:

1. She flumped.
2. It was a garzatious zimper.
3. The flittle wouldn't grantinate.
4. She flumped when the zimper would not grantinate.

Again, is that reading? I hope you answer no, although this does remind me of certain tests we've all taken. Does your definition of reading "work" when applied to the sentence about the flittle?
Let's look at another definition of reading:

Reading is a precise process. It involves exact, detailed, sequential perception and identification of letters, words, spelling patterns, and larger language units. (View denounced by Goodman, 1967, p. 126)

Is that how you read? Do you move from the little details to the larger units as you read? Let's see. Read this sentence:

Although they had been introduced at the dance on Saturday, she didn't remember Yirachmeal Braschicz's name when she saw him in class on Monday.

What did you do when you came to that name? Well, first off, you probably understood that it was a name. You didn't tell yourself, "Oh, here's a proper noun. I sometimes skip those and just say, 'the Y-B-person' if the name is difficult to pronounce." Instead, you intuitively used what you know and do with language. That's because you don't only rely on sounds when we read. You intuitively act on Yirachmeal Braschicz as a proper noun; in other words, you use grammar as a cue or window to get at meaning. You probably used the uppercase letters in Yirachmeal Braschicz as another clue. You did all this quite quickly.

Perhaps you thought that, because this is a book on phonics and reading, you'd better sound out the whole name. Good luck with that. The point is that readers do not always or even necessarily begin with some bits of sounds to make meaning. Need more proof of this? Give a first grader who loves dinosaurs a book about those animals. You'll be stunned as the child reads *stegosaurus* and other names of dinosaurs as you stumble through those pronunciations (at least if you're like me you stumble). How can kids read "Pokémon"? Do you think they rely on each little part, or have they experienced Pokémon as a whole and meaningful unit and learned to read it as such?

Reading is not a precise process. It involves much ambiguity and even guesswork (Goodman, 1967). Then again, maybe you like definitions that rely on the sequences of sounds of letters and think they serve us well in understanding what beginning readers do. Perhaps you're convinced that beginning readers should be taught to focus on letters (or sounds), then words, and then progressively larger bits of language. The issue needs to be: What is the place of phonics in a reading instruction program? But we can't get at this fully until we understand the place of phonics in the act of reading. We can't get to that until we have a definition of reading.

How's your definition holding up so far? Let's push it a little more. . . .

MORE DEFINITIONS OF READING

Consider another definition. Now don't get bored with these! It is very important that you get a sense of the broadness of the field of definitions of reading. Then when we return to Karen's class to analyze what is going on there, you can do so in a more informed manner.

The [structural] linguist's concept of reading is not the concept commonly held by the classroom teacher and the reading specialist—that reading is

getting meaning from the print on a page. The [structural] linguist con-
ceives the reading act as that of turning the stimulus of the graphic shapes
on a surface back into speech. The shapes represent speech; meaning is not
found in the marks but in the speech, which the marks represent. (Strickland, 1964, p. 10)

In order to comprehend what [she or] he reads, the reader turns the visual
stimulus of written language back into speech—overtly if he is inexperienced
and immature, subliminally if he is a rapid, experienced reader. (Strickland,
1964, pp. 13–14; cited in Weaver, 1994, p. 9)

Do readers turn written language back to oral language? This would imply
that written language is talk written down. But it's not. I'll show you. Right
now, as I write, my daughter is in the background, on the phone. I can't hear
what the caller is saying, but I can hear her. Here's what she is saying (I'll put
a dash [—] before each of her turns to speak):

—umm-hmm
—yes, she was going to the st …
—yeah
—I wanted to, but I had too much …
—yeah, I hate that. I didn't even know we had any.
—You did? Is yours done?

Do you notice how many turns get interrupted? You'd rarely see such a
conversation written down. When writers write, say a story about a teen-
ager on the phone, they need to put in many different things than simply
the words that were said. They describe the location, the relationships, the
way things and people look, and much more. Written language is very different from oral language because when someone speaks to you (even on
the phone), you get a lot of nonverbal information. If you still doubt me,
transcribe your teaching or conversations with a friend. Even transcribe a
story you are telling (not reading) to someone. You'll see how different
written and oral language are because the transcription loses much of what
was present during the oral language event.

Here's another definition. Good luck with it:

Printing is a visual means of representing the sounds, which are language.
Meaning is in these sounds. We want to equip the child to turn the written
words into a spoken word (whether he actually utters it or not) so he will

hear what it says, that is get its meaning . . . we have never found anybody who did not think that the purpose of reading was to get the meaning. The only possible defense of skipping sound and going directly from print to meaning would be that printed words are directly meaningful—that the printed word *green* means the color, but this is not so. It is the spoken word green that designates the color, while the printed word designates the sound of the spoken word. Various [structural] linguistics specialists have recently been stressing this fact. (Walcutt & McCracken, 1970, p. xiv; cited in Weaver, 1994, p. 9 [cited only as from the Teacher's Edition of the *Lippincott Basic Reading, 1975* series])

Well, I'm confused. Does this mean that there is no green paint in a can of paint until I say the word "green" aloud? Does it mean that we can only name things when we say them aloud? If this were true, I'd never be able to understand a story about *Yirachmeal Braschicz* until I could say his name; well, that's what I think McCracken and Walcutt meant. What do you think they mean? Which leads me to wonder, if you can't tell me what they mean, did you really *read* the selection? Is saying the words aloud *reading* if you don't understand? I'm voting **no** on that last question.

I think this next one is about grammar:

Corresponding to the auditory analysis of sentences the skill of reading can be viewed as the ability to extract from a *visual* signal the underlying struc-ture of the sentences. (Bever & Bower, 1966, p. 20; cited in Weaver, 1988)

As you read, were you able to "extract from a *visual* signal the underly-ing structure of the sentences"? I wonder if this means that we have to dia-gram every sentence we read, either on scrap paper or somewhere in our mind, to understand it. Do you wonder why some reading researchers write this way? I do. I also wonder how such definitions are rendered into classroom practices through prescribed curriculum.

K. Goodman has been criticized for telling teachers they didn't have to teach phonics. As I said in an earlier chapter, he never said that. Here's his definition of reading. Again, hold it up against your own:

Reading is a psycholinguistic guessing game. It involves an interaction be-tween thought and language. Efficient reading does not result from precise perception and identification of all elements, but from skill in selecting the fewest, most productive cues necessary to produce guesses which are right the first time. The ability to anticipate that which has not been seen, of course, is vital in reading, just as the ability to anticipate what has not yet been heard is vital to listening. (K. Goodman, 1967, p. 47)

I like this one. It has been further refined (K. Goodman, 1996), but the older one captures the essence of what readers do. Sorry if your state does not agree with me or your principal won't support me or hire me to do an inservice at your school. Some states are limiting professional development to programs that reflect the definition of reading in the mandated program Karen is using.

After teaching primary children for many years, and now as a researcher myself, K. Goodman's definition works well for me. I like the one I wrote at the beginning of this chapter. Actually, I prefer to put them together. Goodman presented the idea that readers do the least they need to do to get at the meaning they need to make. Reading involves guessing or predicting what will come ———. Then we confirm our predictions. (Yeah, **"next."** I didn't even need to write it, did I?) You could tell what word was coming, and there weren't any letters there to help you sound it out. Some readers' eyes might have jumped to the next line, predicting that there would be more information there. If you did that, you saw "next" and plugged it into the blanks without even going back to reread. So sometimes we don't even read from left to right.

THE BEAT GOES ON . . .
STILL MORE DEFINITIONS!

The question of what reading is has gotten more complicated since 1988 when Weaver did her research. In the 1996 edition of the *Handbook of Reading Research, Volume II* (Barr, Kamil, Mosenthal, & Pearson), there is an entire section called "Constructs of Reader Process," in which the arguments continue about just what reading is. Here are a few of the conflicting definitions from that source:

> Although the concept of sight reading implies one way to read words, it is apparent from our developmental view that different processes may be involved, depending upon the phase of development. All students learn to read words by sight, with mature readers reading sight words more effectively than immature readers. (Ehri, 1996, p. 411)

Do you agree? How does this compare to your definition?

In another chapter, Daneman (1996) wrote:

> One general conclusion that emerges from the literature is that word recognition ability alone cannot account for why some readers are better than others; the processes involved in comprehending and "absorbing" the text meaning are important determinants of reading success, too. (p. 32)

To elaborate the definition of reading just a little more, Vellutino and Denckla (1996) suggested that:

> Research evidence suggests that while adult skilled readers most often use semantically and syntactically based vehicles for word identification, they are able to use phonologically based vehicles as well. Such evidence is consistent with the possibility that developing readers must have both vehicles for word identification in order to acquire any degree of fluency in reading. (p. 604)

In that same lengthy volume, Stanovich (1996), argued that: "Word recognition remains the central subprocess of the complex act of reading" (p. 442).

One final word from that same volume in a chapter by Paris, Wasik, and Turner (1996):

> Twenty years ago, the development of skilled reading was viewed as a linear accumulation of skills. When children were developmentally ready, they learned sound-symbol correspondence, followed by sight words and decoding, followed by interpretation of sentences and text. This reductionistic and additive model of learning has been challenged by researchers and educators. . . . An overemphasis on elementary skills led to repeated practice with decontextualized language and isolated component skills. Neither teachers nor students enjoy reading and writing in approaches that emphasize skills at the expense of meaningful involvement with text. (p. 634)

This definition captures the loss of joy that Karen and her students are experiencing. What is the role of joy in your definition of reading?

Different definitions of reading continue to make their presence known. In one of the most prestigious research journals on reading, the *Reading Research Quarterly*, the first issue of the new century (Readence & Barone, 2000) contains five different understandings of what reading is (Cunningham, Many, Carver, Gunderson, and Mosenthal). What often saddens teachers like Karen is that teachers' definitions don't seem to count for much, although Karen, a teacher with 20 years of experience, has taught many children to read proficiently.

CATEGORIES ACROSS DEFINITIONS

Willis (1997) looked across the many years of reading research and found three categories into which many definitions of reading fit. One category views reading (she uses the broader term *literacy*, but I refer mostly to reading) as a skill. In this category are the researchers who discuss reading as a collection of specific abilities or procedures that when mastered or enacted support success not only in reading, but in the greater economic, social, and political spheres in which one lives. Simply put, if you collect the skills, you will meet success.

The second category that Willis (1997) found is one she referred to as "literacy-as-school-knowledge" (p. 389). This means that knowing how to read involves reading the word and also understanding the world of school so that one will succeed in school with this very specific school-based knowledge of reading. Children who know how to sit, behave, engage in the kinds of conversations that are typical of school settings, and do their work will meet with success in school. Children who do well with "literacy-as-school-knowledge" are the ones who do well on tests in school situations.

The third category that Willis (1997) presented is "literacy as a social and cultural construct" (p. 391). This is a view of reading that involves reading the word and the world (Freire & Macedo, 1987) and pays attention to the social and political (and hence economic) complexities that are part of what it means to teach reading, learn to read, and engage in increased awareness that accompanies being literate. This last view is one I'll return to in the chapter on politics and reading. Think about your definition of reading and where it fits in Willis' categories.

I know that so far this chapter has in it many quotes from other reading researchers. I included these voices to demonstrate just how complicated things about reading are. We are the consumers of this research when we buy a reading program, engage with children and texts provided by those programs, send our loved ones to schools that mandate such programs, or take a stance about what reading is and how it might best be taught. When teachers are ordered to do something in their classrooms, they are agents for (through that order) someone's definition of reading. By "agents for" I mean that the teachers may not agree with the program, but by delivering it to the children (following the district mandates) they become technicians responsible for the delivery of the implicit definition of reading that the program expresses. Let's look more closely at the definition of reading at work in this program.

THE PHONICS PROGRAM'S DEFINITION
OF READING

Experience builds meaning and knowledge. This means that when we experience things, those experiences contribute to or influence other experiences that help us figure out what is going on around us and assign meaning to it. We learn how to live in certain places (including schools) by learning what the rules are, what things are called, and acceptable ways to act based on our learning. For example, when I moved to New Mexico, I didn't understand the server in a local restaurant. I'd ordered a meal and he asked, "Red or green?"

"What do you mean?" I asked.

He was quite understanding. "You're new to New Mexico, aren't you?" he asked.

"Well, yes," I half mumbled, embarrassed at not knowing an aspect of local dining culture.

"Whenever you order food in restaurants in New Mexico, servers will ask you if you want red or green chile on your entrée."

"How do I know which one to ask for?" I asked.

"First ask which one is hotter. It's different at different restaurants. Then decide how hot you want the topping on your food to be."

Sometimes we aren't taught so directly, but we usually figure out how to be successful in school. For example, if you are a student attending the first session of a class, you have certain expectations. You expect to learn what the instructor expects, but you have certain broad expectations about being in the course. You expect the course to be in a specific language, and you expect that language to be used in a certain way. You'd be surprised if the instructor used many expletives and disappointed if the instructor used many words you hadn't heard before. As the instructor speaks, you learn many things aside from what the course expectations are as written on the syllabus. You learn if she or he has a sense of humor; if he or she is flexible; if he or she likes to negotiate assignments; if she or he allows or encourages class members to participate; if you're supposed to raise your hand; if the instructor is balding or has warts. All this information is learned with little direct instruction. As the course sessions proceed, you learn about how the class is going to "be." You learn if it will be lecture, conversational, and so on. Overall, you are learning about learning as you learn about the content of the course, the context for the learning, and the rules within that context.

Now let's consider Karen's classroom. Operationally, there are definitions of reading in place at every moment of every day in every classroom. The children know and name what they are doing as *reading*, even when Karen calls it phonics. The child who read the <h> poster to me knew she was reading it. Looking operationally means that the definition of reading is something that is visible in the classroom via the activity that is going on. We consider the activity, the things used during the activity, and the ways in which the participants act and interact as leading to the definition (Spradley, 1980). When researchers develop a theory based on what they see, it is called a *grounded theory* (Glaser & Strauss, 1967). We can develop a grounded definition of reading by studying what is occurring when children are learning to read. A grounded definition is one that is built by considering what is in operation.

This means that in the daily activities within a classroom, a teacher is teaching children what reading is, what it means, how it works, and how it is used. It means that any program we use is teaching children these same things. Although Karen would not call the time that her children engaged in phonics *reading*, she is reading during the entire lesson. She reads from the script provided by the publisher. The children watch her reading, they respond to her reading, and they learn about what reading is in school. For example, after the phonics lesson, they talked about reading the book that Karen passed out to them on one piece of paper, reading the words they made from cards, and reading the words she wrote on the markerboard. The children see it all as reading.

This means that reading is many things. The phonics program presents learning to read as separate from reading to learn (Short, 1999). Karen believes that children learn to read and read to learn at the same time. Her side trip to the real book about dinosaurs and the many strategies she uses during other times of the day demonstrate that belief. But for the full hour that the phonics program is delivered to her students, they are learning that being a reader means saying little bits of language as isolated sounds. Let's take a closer look at the definition of reading they are constructing.

PHONICS LESSONS TEACH
WHAT READING IS

The lesson began with a "you blend" story. In this activity, reading is operationally defined as the blending together of sounds. The focus on saying the sounds, getting them right, and moving on to the next set of sounds detracts from any focus on meaning. This is further evidenced by the lack of any substantive discussion of the story.

The lesson continued with a sudden shift to the markerboard and the use of real words to produce nonwords. Consider the children's responses when they change superman to supermad. Some of the children urge Karen and their colleagues to make the words make sense. They provide ideas for what supermad might mean. Interestingly, the children who do this are the ones that Karen has identified as already being proficient readers. The other children in the class observe their colleagues' struggle for meaning-making, some join in, while others do not participate in the struggle. The proficient readers demand meaning here and at other points in the same activity. Do you remember the child asking, "What is 'supermand'?" Karen tells the child it is not a word. I am suggesting that this sends a confusing message to children. It tells them that reading is saying words even if you don't understand them. The lesson is demonstrating to the children that when we engage in reading the goal is to call the sounds—to blend them.

Now consider the change from baboon to baboot. This is an instance when there is no discussion among the children or between the children and Karen. Karen presents the real word, it is read by strong readers, it is changed to a nonword, it is called by someone, and she moves on. I know that teachers and children cannot spend each second of each day analyzing every instance of instructional activity. However, I submit that the compliance of the children in saying the word indicates that they are subscribing to the implicit definition of reading at hand. They are buying into the notion that reading is saying the nonword the teacher presents. They defer to the teacher and incorporate what is enacted during the lesson as the stuff of reading. Schools rely on children being "good" and participating in lessons politely. Children learn a lot by doing so. In this case, they are learning what reading is at this point during the day. They are learning that reading lacks sense.

ISOLATING SOUNDS AND WORDS— NO CONTEXTS/NO MEANING

Karen brings out the puppet during the next part of the lesson. Sniggle teaches the children to listen for the ending sounds of words. The children are asked to repeat the final consonant sounds of each word the puppet says, but this is just not always possible. For example, think of the word "eat," one of the words the children heard Sniggle say. How would you isolate the sound of the <t> in "eat"? It's very difficult to say this without adding the sound of a short vowel. Most children say "tuh," which will not always help them pronounce a word they don't know. The children who can already read are successful at this activity. The children who are struggling or not yet reading are not gaining from this activity (Vernon & Ferreiro, 1999).

The isolation of a single consonant sound remains problematic with the move to the <d> part of the lesson. Very few adults or children can pronounce a /d/ in isolation. The insertion of an extra vowel sound is natural and may also contribute to confusion on the part of a beginning or struggling reader. Practicing the sounds of /d/ by saying "duh duh" for the sound of a dinosaur's large feet is not helpful to beginning readers (Moustafa, 1997).

When the children experience word families in the phonics program, exposures are brief and focused more on individual letter sounds than common endings or beginnings. The changes from dad to had to mad are quick, as dictated by the teachers guide. When Karen has time, she focuses more closely on such a family, specific to the needs of small groups or individual children rather than delivering this to all (some of whom may not need it). Her definition of reading as rooted in meaning is expressed in activities that Karen develops and uses with her students. When she uses those that are developed by the phonics program authors, her definition of reading with its focus on meaning is deferred.

Karen knows that isolated sounds or lists of words presented to readers are less meaningful than the use of words from meaningful contexts. When she has time, she works with selected students using big books that have interesting stories in them. She and the children discuss the stories and eventually work toward word study and sound study. She always begins with meaningful text as a context for studying isolated sounds. She uses onsets and rimes (which is like studying word families) whenever possible because of the research that shows that children learn phonics most effectively this way (Moustafa, 1997).

LIMITING LEARNING

The move to the playing cards, which the children just love to handle and pretend to play real card games with, is also significant. Recall that one child wanted to make "candy," but needed a <y> and knew he needed that letter. Other children did not understand the activity so they did what their colleagues did with the cards to get the right answer. The program assumes a clear playing field. It assumes that all the children are in the same place and need the same lesson at the same time. Over the course of the school year, the lesson is that all children get the same thing at the same time in the same order or sequence and at the same rate. It presumes or allows for little or no differences between children. It takes (robs, usurps) at least a full hour each day.

This leveling of the field is a problem for Karen because she knows that children in first grade develop differently, and that there comes a point in the year when children just "take off" (Cochran, Cochran, Scalena, & Buchanan, 1985) as readers. This program is holding some children back and pushing some children too hard. It is teaching children that reading is the same for all, all the time. It is teaching that you learn to read from the teacher, and that the child's mind can only do, as a reader, what the teacher has taught. However, this is just not true. Children know a lot about language; when that knowledge is honored, they can use it to become powerful readers without a systematic intense and extremely controlled scope and sequence (Smith, 1985). Karen has seen this happen for years as a first-grade teacher.

When I was a graduate student, Yetta Goodman told us a story about her work with a struggling fifth-grade reader. She spoke with the child and over the course of a year got to know him. One day, she gave the student a book with no words in it and asked the child to read it. We were amazed to hear that the child stuttered and sputtered, as if he was trying to sound out words, when there were no words in the book. He only had to tell a story to go along with the illustrations. The point is that the child had learned that reading was supposed to sound like someone gagging through sounds. Some of Karen's students are learning that too, except that Karen spends much of the rest of her day trying to compensate for the hours she gives to phonics.

LIMITING READERS

The closing part of the lesson is profound in its teaching of what reading is. The story about the cat who would nap in the mat, in the pan . . . well, you get the idea, is teaching some of the children that reading is saying phonetically regular words. This means that they are learning that reading is not necessarily telling good stories (and everything else that reading can be).

Lynn Rhodes (1981) told the story of her work with a child who spent a lot of time writing a story at an after-school clinic for struggling readers and writers. When she showed it to Lynn, it read, "I had a cat." Engaging the child in conversation about the story, Lynn learned that the child never had a cat, but the child wrote the story because it was the only one she thought she could **spell**. The child was in an intensive phonics program in school and worried more about spelling her story correctly than having it be meaningful. Such programs teach children that stories must always be put on paper with great accuracy at the phonic level even if this involves disregarding meaning (and reality—the child did not have a cat!). Thus, limiting children as readers limits them as writers.

Young children know that adults are more competent than children in many ways with words. However, children in phonics-dominated classrooms may be developing a deficit-based identity in terms of their competence as readers (Martens, 1996). If they have an increasingly limited access to fine literature that they can read, they get the message that fine literature is off limits for them. They might see their teacher reading the good books, but the children don't have access to them. When you add socioeconomic differences into this formula, it becomes more ominous because children with limited books in their homes are now experiencing limiting definitions of reading in their school lives. Karen is fighting to keep a literature base in her classroom and to maintain children's access to literature. Still, the hour of phonics creates an ambiguous message about what reading is.

Children can live with ambiguity. Reading is ambiguous by nature. Children are resilient, too. Yet why would we want to set them up this way, confusing their understanding of what reading is? Why would we want to draw such strong lines between the stories children read and those that they hear their teacher or other readers read? The sooner children feel like readers, the sooner they will engage in reading the way I defined it at the beginning of this chapter. If they feel outside of the literacy club (Smith, 1988), they cannot participate in it as real readers. If children do not have experiences with texts that allow them to closely approximate what Karen does as a reader, they may not develop definitions of reading that include themselves as legitimate readers.

In the program that Karen is using, the definition of reading is consistent with that of Flesch (1955), who suggested that if you teach children the sounds that letters make and how they go together, then the children are reading when they put the sounds together and say them. One part of this program that I did not discuss Karen doing involves writing letters on the board, one at a time, and saying to the class, "Sound, sound, blend . . ." (I saw other teachers do this part of the phonics program). For example, a teacher might write <s> and say, "sound." The class says "/s/." Leaving the <s> on the board, she adds, <a> and says, "sound." Then the children say, "/a/." Then the teacher says, "blend," and the children say the sounds together /sa/, as in "sat." The procedure continues with the addition of <t>, at which point the children are told to say the sound (/t/) and then blend the entire word, to say, "sat." This is another example of the vigilant focus on the sounds of letters that is the cornerstone of the definition of reading in this program.

SHORT /a/ ISN'T TOO RELIABLE

When you work with words in isolation, you are teaching children what reading is as much as when you read books to them. If they don't know what the words mean, you are teaching them that reading is nonsense (Smith, 1985). If you try to standardize sounds that in real life vary quite a bit, you are teaching them that reading is unfamiliar sounds. Let's examine a little more closely the sound of <a> in the lesson. Some of the words used in the lesson were: <u>nap</u>, <u>mat</u>, <u>pan</u>, <u>pad</u>, <u>cap</u>, <u>and</u>, <u>hand</u>, and <u>can't</u>. I argue that the sound of <a> is different in some of these. An <a> followed by an <n> sounds different than an <a> followed by a <p>. The nasal sound of /n/ affects the sound of the <a>. Thus, although you might think these are all very regular words, they're not quite that regular.

Short /a/ is just not that reliable when it comes in contact with a variety of letters. That is why it is more effective to teach word families such as the -an family: can, fan, man, pan, and so on.

To confuse things just a little more, the sounds of many of the letters change with dialect or region of the country. Yet there's more to add to the confusion. Did you notice that you have to look **past** the /a/ to know what sound it will make? If the /a/ is followed by an /r/ or /im/ or /che/, it makes very different sounds than if it is followed by /d/ or /t/. Hmmmm, maybe reading is not as left to right as some thought.

Dorothy Watson (personal communication), a well-known reading researcher and teacher educator, tells the story of a struggling reader who sat in a group of children to whom Dorothy was reading. Dorothy recalled reading to the children, holding the book up as she read so that the children could see the illustrations while they listened. One of the struggling readers asked her, "How do you do that?"

"How do I do what?" Dorothy asked.

"How do you read with your ear?"

The child thought that because the book was alongside Dorothy's head as she read, the secret to reading must have to do with the ears as well as the eyes. Children are constantly looking for the keys to unlock some mystery to learning to read, especially if they are beginning or struggling. We've got to consider every one of our teaching actions as directly related to how they solve that mystery. I'm not saying that we should not hold up books as we read. Rather, we need to tell children what we are doing and why. This means we need to understand what we are doing and why. This means we have to make clear and conscious choices of what we are doing in our teaching, based in our definition of reading.

ARE YOU SAYING NEVER TEACH PHONICS?

No. I'm saying that if teachers are informed about reading, like Karen, they can decide what to teach, how much, how often, and to whom. I want to help you decide which phonics rules or generalizations to teach. First, a little history.

When Theodore Clymer was a primary grade teacher in the early 1960s, he taught his students many phonics lessons (reprinted in Clymer, 1996). One of his students asked if phonics rules were all that useful because it seemed that every time Clymer presented a rule, he also presented some exceptions to the rule. The child wanted to know why he bothered teaching the rules if they were saturated with exceptions. The question intrigued Clymer, so he took his teacher's guides and listed all the generalizations that he was directed to teach. There were 45 of them. He then chose a percentage of times that he would want the generalization to work for it to be truly useful to the young readers in his class.

What number would you choose as the percentage of times that a generalization would work before you'd teach it? Really, go on, pick a number. Write it right on this line: __%. OK? That's the percentage of times that a rule or generalization should work before you'd teach it.

Clymer chose a number, too. He chose 75% as the cutoff number. He wanted a rule to work 75% of the time before he'd teach it. Of the 45 generalizations he studied, only 18 worked at the level he demanded. The rest fell far below.

You can read this study; it was reprinted in *The Reading Teacher* (Clymer, 1996). There's a hitch! When Clymer studied the generalizations, he applied them to the basal reading program he was using in his own classroom. He listed all the words in the basal and found which rule each word was supposed to fit. So, even in the basal, where authors and publishers were supposed to be very careful to ensure that all the words were regular, the generalizations didn't hold water. What would have happened if Clymer went into authentic texts to find if the generalizations worked? He would have found them to be even less trustworthy. Yet his students still learned to read. That's because they used all the cueing systems, not just phonics.

Let's play with this idea of phonics generalizations and their usefulness. Take the number that is the percentage of times that you want a phonics generalization to work (you wrote it earlier). In the appendix, I list the rules that Clymer was supposed to teach his children, but I do so in a playful way. The appendix is a sort of quiz in which you find words that fit the generalizations and words that don't. Then you guess how often the generalization works (in the form of a percentage). Then you decide if you'd teach the generalization to students in your class. You might photocopy the "test" and give it to parents who want you to teach phonics. Also use it to consider what you want to teach and why. Use it as a way to think about other ways (such as those described by Moustafa, 1997, or Pinnell & Fountas, 1998) to teach children about the relationships among letters, sounds, and words in such a way that you honor your definition of reading. The point of the appendix is that readers (like you) don't need to know or be able to state rules in order to read.

YOUR THOUGHTS

Did you change or adjust your definition of reading? If so, how? How did you learn to read? How do you feel about reading? How did your attitudes about reading develop? Who influenced you? How? Do you remember the day you learned short /a/? What kind of reader are you? How do you use reading? What's it for in your life? How do your responses to these questions reflect the way you learned to read and the ways you think reading should be taught? I hope you can discuss these questions with colleagues.

As you turn to chapter 4, consider what you believe teachers' roles to be in the classroom. Consider the decisions that Karen made before the phonics mandate and after it.

4

Phonics Programs,
Teacher Knowledge,
and Teacher Identity

now thread my voice
with lies of lightness
force within
my mirror eyes
the cold disguise
of sad and wise
decisions.
　　　　　　—"How I Can Lie To You" by Maya Angelou (1971, p. 17)

SAD AND WISE DECISIONS

Many decisions were made leading to the adoption of the phonics program
that Karen is being forced to use. On the surface, the decision is to have a
phonics program in place to support children's reading. However, the decision is just not that simple. The program that was selected, the way it is being mandated, and the experiences that children and teachers have each day
in school all suggest many more decisions. Decisions have been made about
the definition of reading, and inherent in that definition are decisions about
what children will do in school, what the teacher knows and can do, where
knowledge comes from (a publisher via a district office or other sources),
curriculum, and how teachers use time in school. So one decision is many
decisions in a single disguise—a phonics program.

INFORMED AND FRUSTRATED TEACHING

In this chapter, I look closely at Karen. I want to acknowledge that looking closely at Karen involves my representing her to you. This means that I analyze the teaching Karen did in her classroom and what happened to her within, around, and because of her teaching. Brueggeman (1996) wrote that "there was no way by the end of my fieldwork that I felt I could neatly separate out my personal and professional roles and feelings" (p. 31). Knowing Karen, I felt the same way and wanted her as a partner in this work. The sad part is that Karen cannot participate as a co-author of this chapter or book. It falls to me to present her to you. My goal is to present her in a way that is indicative of the great respect that I hold for her as a teacher, thinker, and decision maker. I hope that you, as a reader, find my representation of her to be clear, fair, and not presumptuous.

Karen's knowledge of reading research is quite sound. She earned a master's degree, attends national and international reading conferences, is well read in professional journals about reading, and is reflective about her practice. Karen's knowledge, expressed as teaching decisions she makes, is systematically discounted when she is pressured into using the phonics program with her entire class.

Let's return to Karen's classroom for a moment. Karen recounts, after her students leave for lunch,

> I was told by [the district reading administrator] that for too long teachers in this district have thought that their job was to create curriculum. I was told that is not our job. Our job is to "deliver" [she makes quote signs in the air with her fingers] curriculum.

Karen's frustration is *informed* frustration. She is not frustrated because of vague feelings she has. Her frustration lies in being informed about the reading process but **not** being able to make informed decisions about her teaching because of the dogmatic nature of the prescribed curriculum. She is not able to make informed decisions that would benefit her students' learning because of the scripted lessons. It is not that she doesn't *like* or plan to teach phonics. Rather her frustration is rooted in the knowledge that her professional decision making is appropriated. She can no longer decide which strategies to use to address learning needs she identifies in her ongoing assessments of her students.

CONSTRUCTIVISM

The idea of *teacher-as-thinker* is expressed in some of the professional literature as *constructivism*.

> Constructivism refers to the belief that human knowledge is constructed within the minds of individuals and within social communities; and the bodies of knowledge that inform individuals as well as their means of acquisition are themselves human constructions. (Richardson, 1999, p. 146)

The view of the *teacher-as-knowledge-constructor* is in direct opposition to the view of the teacher as an empty vessel to be filled, often called the transmission or banking model of learning (Freire, 1970a).

What is at work here is a fundamental difference between Karen (and teachers like her) and her district regarding the view of how teachers learn and what teachers can know. The district believes that Karen and her children can know what the district tells them. Karen is viewed as a knower who can only know what some supposedly more knowledgeable knower can deliver to her. Richardson (1999) suggested that such a view is limiting and does not honor recent research on teachers and teaching:

> The cognitive revolution has changed our thinking about teaching and teacher education by focusing on cognition, beliefs, and the making of meaning as the desired outcomes of interest rather than, or in addition to, prescribed skills and behaviors. (p. 145)

Richardson suggested that teachers still need to learn skills. I agree. The important "and" here is that teachers learn skills *and* they also are thoughtful meaning- and knowledge-makers.

Teacher knowledge, from a constructivist perspective, is not something that exists to deflate the power of district offices. The ultimate goal is children's enhanced learning:

> The capacity of teachers and other educators to deeply understand teaching and learning, to produce and use knowledge on behalf of their practice, I would argue, is central to the realization of a genuine right to learn. [This stands in contrast to] efforts to deskill and control teaching by limiting both teachers' autonomy and their level of education. (Darling-Hammond, 1996, p. 10)

WHAT KAREN KNOWS

Karen knows that there is an increasing knowledge base in reading (Braunger & Lewis, 1997) that is not present in the mandated phonics program. The issue here is teachers' knowledge. We need to consider not only the many things Karen knows about reading, but also the views others have of that knowledge. Specifically, the district is acting (as evidenced by the mandated phonics program) as if teacher knowledge is something that teachers should be "trained" in. The idea of being "trained" comes from behavioral views of psychology and learning. Hoffman and Pearson (2000) discussed training this way:

> Training sits alongside a set of other interactive approaches, such as conditioning, instructing, and indoctrinating . . . [Training] will not help teachers develop the personal and professional commitment to lifelong learning required by those teachers who want to confront the complexities and contradictions of teaching . . . training is equally as insufficient and complete as a model for preparing readers. (p. 36)

Training, then, is not sufficient for teachers or students. Teachers who are trained in the delivery of phonics programs are being given "knowledge-for-practice" (Cochran-Smith & Lytle, 2000). This is knowledge that is delivered from some outside source to the teachers for use in classrooms. There are certainly times when teachers need this type of knowledge. However, a training-oriented view of teachers' knowledge does not take into account that teachers also have knowledge that they discover *in* their classrooms and knowledge that they construct *for* their classrooms (Cochran-Smith & Lytle, 2000). Knowledge *in* is knowledge that teachers discover; knowledge *for* is knowledge that teachers construct. Another way of looking at this is that teachers, as thinkers and learners, are inventors of classrooms (Whitmore & Crowell, 1994), along with their children. A view of teachers as empty and in need of "training" denies the process of invention that is so crucial to the complexity of life in schools in which children's needs must be addressed.

Districts that hire constructivist teachers are getting "empowered teachers who are in control of their own thinking and actions" (Hoffman & Pearson, 2000, p. 37). In a text for preservice teachers, Templeton (1995) expressed the hope that he has for constructivist teachers of reading:

It is clear, therefore, that teaching children to read . . . may be the single most important responsibility you have as an elementary-school teacher. Because you will be *reflective*, *critical*, and *creative* with your teaching of reading, your students should be that way in assimilating what they learn. To prosper and grow in peace and in hope, the very society of which they are a part will need both this type of understanding and individuals who will act, with compassion and commitment, on the basis of it. (p. 30; italics added)

Karen admits feeling somewhat disappointed because she thought her district expected her to be knowledgeable and thoughtful. The push for developmentally appropriate practice was accompanied by much talk about constructivism. Now all the decisions, including the words she will say, are scripted for her, and her thinking must be deferred to scripts in teachers' guides.

Many researchers are acknowledging and studying the complexity of teachers' thinking. Putnam and Borko (2000) summarized some of the research about how teachers learn "new ways of teaching" (p. 4). They suggested that the "physical and social contexts" are an important part of teacher learning because teachers think about these contexts when designing and carrying out curricular decisions and studies of their own practices. In other words, the differences that teachers see in their classrooms from day to day and year to year are very real and deserving of professional status and prestige. Teaching is site- and child-specific and cannot be addressed with scripts. Teaching is most effective when an informed professional is supported in her decision making. Karen knows this.

Yet there's an interesting twist in the constructivist view of teacher knowledge. Karen knows that not every teacher in her district wants to be a decision maker. She says that

> . . . some teachers thought that children learned by osmosis. They got this idea because when we were trying to become whole language teachers we didn't give each other enough help. Programs like [the phonics program] give teachers some guidelines. They didn't have any guidelines before this. The program gives them a structure that they think gives kids everything they need.

This certainly complicates things. Here is one district in which there is tension because some teachers want to construct curriculum and others want decisions made for them. The administration switched from wanting the former to wanting the latter without addressing the tension between two kinds of teachers: thinkers-as-a-decision-maker and followers-of-the-decisions-of-others.

APPROPRIATING TEACHERS' DECISION MAKING

Karen's definition of reading has been appropriated by the district and administrators at her school through the decisions they made. Karen can still think, cry, and discuss, but she feels she cannot change what others are demanding must be covered in her classroom. Her decision making has been overshadowed, her thinking marginalized, and her professionalism confiscated. This goes beyond discussions of what reading is, how children learn to read, and how it is we come to know what we know about reading. It moves to the nature of teaching, the role of the teacher, and the teachers' role in decisions about and enactment of curriculum.

Karen and some other teachers in the district refer to "they" when the teachers discuss the phonics program that is being instituted. The teachers say things like, "They are making us . . ."; "they are forcing us . . ."; "they are watching us." "They" are the district reading administrator, some assistant superintendents for instruction and evaluation, and other district personnel. These personnel visited the schools during the first year of the phonics program's presence in the district. The district personnel met with teachers after school, visited classrooms during the school day, and worked with school-site administrators to reinforce the importance of following the phonics program. The pressure was on, and the administrators and teachers were responding. This flurry of district activity was based on reading test scores. That is high-stakes testing. Do you see what's at stake? One answer to that question is this: teachers' minds. Teachers' professional decision making is another answer.

INTIMIDATION

Karen and I discussed some of the district-sponsored meetings about the phonics program. She told me that during these meetings, teachers asked questions of the "they" and of representatives of the phonics program.

"We were also told," Karen explains, "that teachers in this district have acted as though they are self-employed and that they are not self-employed and they need to stop acting as though they are."

"What does that mean?" I ask her.

"It means," Karen's eyes once again fill with tears, "that we are not allowed to think for ourselves or make decisions."

It means teachers will follow the mandate or find other employment.

It means that Karen's understanding of reading is dismissed, and that in this district there is one definition of reading reflected in a single view of reading instruction. The district is so committed to this view of reading instruction that no children are allowed to leave the classroom during this time. The ESL, Reading Recovery, special needs, and gifted students all must remain in Karen's classroom for phonics; thus, they are often pulled out when the remnants of Karen's holistic program are enacted. Five or more of her students often leave for work with specialists when she has time for big books and other activities.

"I wonder what the justification is for having the kids stay and all sit through the same lesson?" I ask.

Before I finish the sentence, Karen shakes her head. "I didn't believe this! We were at a district inservice about this program and someone asked that very question. The company representative said, 'Trust me. This program is good for every child in your class.' "

"The last time someone said 'trust me,' " I say, "I wound up buying a Chevy Nova."

We both only half laugh.

Teaching that is grounded in substantive thinking (Shannon, 1989) is based on research, classroom experience, knowledge of the children, knowledge of the community, and relationships with colleagues. Karen's teaching has historically been based on her substantive thinking about what her children are doing, what she knows they need, their interests, her interests, the interests of the families of the children, and national goals (National Council of Teachers of English/International Reading Association, 1996). She usually found ways to bring families into the curriculum and into the school. She has been an expert at helping children get excited about their learning because she is an outstanding kidwatcher (Goodman, 1985). When Yetta Goodman explains what kidwatchers do, she is describing Karen.

Kidwatching is not just looking at children; kidwatching is having the information, knowledge, understanding, and thoughtfulness to act on what it is that one is observing. Kidwatchers have "current knowledge about child language and conceptual development," and they know that "language and concepts grow and develop depending on the settings in which they occur, the experiences that children have in those settings, and the interaction of the people in those settings" (p. 11). When Karen sighed and said, "It's not for every child," she captured the essence of being a kidwatcher who wants to use what she knows when she teaches. By teaching the scripted program, Karen is a living example of what happens when intimidation paralyzes pedagogy.

COMPLIANCE

Karen was intimidated into complying with the mandate. She needs her job. She loves her job. Her love of children keeps her in teaching despite the massive frustrations she is facing in the more recent years of her career as the district turns its back on the successes of her holistic teaching and learning philosophy. Interestingly, most of the district's classrooms were basal-based when the newspaper reported the scores. That didn't matter. Whole language teaching was held up as the problem and phonics instruction was the cure.

Once the new direction of the district was clear, Karen's principal met with her to encourage her to support the program for its first year. He knew that her response to the program would influence other teachers in the building because of how highly respected she is. Karen acquiesced; she had to. The pressure was on, the direction of the district was apparent, the threats were coming through, and she felt that the choices were clear: Stay and use the program or leave.

With the increase in reading scores following the first year of use of the program, Karen faces another year of implementing the program. But don't be deceived by the scores. They rose on a test that is mimicked by the phonics program. The curriculum taught to the test and taught the children to take the test. Additionally, the district purchased a test preparation program that involved months of practice on items just like those on the test. In fact, the test and the test preparation program are published by the same publisher. Two independent variables (a test preparation program and a phonics program) were at work at the same time. This confounds (invalidates) any statistical reliability as to what influenced the rise in test scores.

That didn't matter.

"Just when I finished phonics for the year, I had to start [the test preparation program]," Karen moans. "They keep getting pieces of my students' school days."

There "they" are again; the "they" to whom Karen must comply. The "they" who take her students' needs and reduce them to one need that can be addressed by the voice of a program.

The success of the phonics programs was hailed and both programs (test preparation and phonics) would be used in subsequent years. "Now the district is looking at basal programs that have more phonics in them, too," Karen sadly recounts. "Scores went up so we are going to get more of the same."

Karen's frustration grows. She works now (in the second year of the mandate) at finding ways to skim through the phonics lessons, ignoring the scripts, but she continues to have the whole class receive the lesson. She knows that she can slip into the script if her principal appears at her door during a lesson. Things will look as they are supposed to look as long as the entire class is seated on the rug. She can attribute her increased speed in lesson delivery to her increased efficacy with and understanding of the program. She decides to reduce lesson time by not doing entire lessons so she can meet the needs of the emerging readers in her class.

Karen and I both know that around the district many teachers continue to comply with the mandated program exactly as it was written. This is borne out when I visit teachers throughout the district. There's that tension, again, about how a teacher can use what she or he knows.

ARE TEACHERS MERELY TECHNICIANS?

The question that nags here is this: What is a teacher supposed to be and do? This leads to other questions. What about teachers like Karen who have read the research on phonics programs like this (G. Coles, 2000; Taylor, 1998) and know such programs are not effective in the teaching of reading? Why are those teachers complying with the district's demands?

Karen and other teachers are frightened. They were intimidated by district personnel and believe that their jobs are at stake. This is probably accurate. A teacher can be fired for insubordination if a district administrator demands the enactment of a specific curriculum and the teacher blatantly disregards that demand. I do not make light of the fear that Karen and others feel. That fear leads to pain because a district-level decision, such as the adoption of a phonics program, and its accompanying intimidation suggests a view of teachers not as substantive thinkers, but as technicians (Shannon, 1989) who cannot make decisions for themselves. Such decisions are systematic deprofessionalizations of teachers.

In another book that I wrote with teachers (Meyer et al., 1998) about the amazing inquiry that their children were doing in the primary grades, I interviewed many teachers at the school where the inquiry was taking place. One of the teachers who was not engaging in classroom-based inquiry with her students explained that her job was not to create curriculum. She believed that her job was to deliver curriculum. Thus, there was a distinct difference in definitions of "teacher" between the groups of teachers at the school. Some believed that teachers were to "do what we are told," as one teacher put it. Others believed that teachers are decision makers who can involve children in the creation of curriculum. One is a view of the teacher as a technician; the other is a view of the teacher as more thoughtful than even a skilled technician.

The deeper difference is a difference in theoretical or philosophical orientation to the profession of teaching. The more conservative view is that teachers are technicians who perpetuate what exists, deliver predetermined and prescribed knowledge to students, sort and rate students constantly, and work to perpetuate the distribution of knowledge and power as it presently exists.

TEACHER SILENCE

Karen's view of the teacher is more progressive than that conservative view. She sees herself as someone who can create curriculum that is specific to the needs and interests of her students and also addresses broader goals and standards (National Council of Teachers of English/International Reading Association, 1996). Yet she remained uncritical—in public—during the first year of the implementation of the phonics program. She did ask questions, however. For example, she asked the representative of the phonics program, "What happens if a child goes through the program and does not learn to read?"

The program representative said, "That never happens."

Karen walked away with that information. Later, enraged, she asked her colleagues how anyone could say such a thing about a program. Her face red and her hands shaking, she said to her colleagues, "to say we should use one program is the farthest thing from the truth that can be."

Even as she saw some negative effects on her students' lives in school, she did not voice her objection to administrators who could make decisions about the program. Silence is a political position into which a person feels forced. Karen felt forced into silence. She felt forced into silence in the same way that the women in Belenky's study (Belenky, Clinchy, Goldberger, & Tarule, 1986) felt forced into silence. Out of fear and constant decisions made without their input (or perhaps with cursory, yet often ignored, input), teachers learn to be silent. That silence manifests itself in compliance to mandates passed down from district offices, principals, and others in perceived or real power positions.

I am not suggesting that Karen should have been the sole voice of opposition to the phonics program. Doing so would have put her in a position of extreme vulnerability. I am saying that historically teachers have not had input, as women they have typically been told to comply (Stuckey, 1991), and that schools are set up in such ways as to perpetuate teacher compliance (and, I suggest in chap. 5 to perpetuate child compliance as well). Lortie (1975) found schools to be cellular in nature, isolating teachers from each other with walls, schedules, talking-head inservices, and discounting of teacher knowledge. When schools are cellular, teachers are insulated from one another, feel alone, and do not talk back to mandates. It's made to seem too risky. It probably is too risky, especially to be a lone voice. This leaves few options for thoughtful teachers. They make a choice, close their doors, and isolate themselves from the larger conversations in which decisions are made. They seek refuge and safety. Silence.

TEACHING IS RELATIONAL

Teachers like Karen threaten district status quo. They are getting increasingly educated by reading, being in study groups, taking courses, doing classroom-based research, and earning advanced degrees. They know that publishers' claims will always be "broken promises" (Shannon, 1989) as long as publishers view teachers as technicians who must unquestioningly follow scripts. Teachers like Karen are not alone. Other educators have thought along the same lines as them, putting children's learning before prescribed programs. Rose (1989) wrote this about his teaching:

> Teaching, I was coming to understand, was a kind of romance. You didn't just work with words or a chronicle of dates or facts. . . . You wooed kids with these things, invited a relationship of sorts, the terms of connection be-

ing the narrative, [an] historical event, [etc.]. Maybe nothing was "intrinsi-
cally interesting." Knowledge gained its meaning, at least initially, through
a touch on the shoulder, through a conversation. (p. 102)

Rose is suggesting that teaching is relational and knowledge-based. I
would go further to say that there is no knowledge without a relationship.
Until I open a book, the text is merely black stuff on a white page. Until I
start to read, the text, although real, is not "knowledge." Knowledge exists
when text or texts (including the texts of conversations) or contexts are engaged by people in relationships. The nature of that relationship is crucial
to the nature of the knowledge. Karen knows this. She knows her relationships with her students are changed so their knowledge is changed when
she spends an hour each day doing phonics.

Deborah Meier (1995), a school principal, wanted the learning community to be respectful of the children's lives, knowledge, and needs. She
wanted the school to be that kind of place for teachers too:

> Schools are the conscious embodiment of the way we want our next genera-
> tion to understand their world and their place in it. It calls upon our most
> critical faculties to sort out what that message ought to be and how the
> teachers who represent the public in this enterprise can embody such ideas.
> If mutual respect is the bedrock condition necessary for a healthy democ-
> racy, then it must be the foundation of schooling. (p. 135)

Karen knows that the phonics program is disrespectful of her students.
Karen is a passionate teacher who could "manage well if all the textbooks,
workbooks, and curricular guides that fill the schools suddenly disappeared" (Perrone, 1991, p. 117). I'm not saying we should rid the school of
every guide or plan. Rather, I am suggesting that teachers like Karen should
be encouraged, not discouraged. They should be held accountable to the
needs of children, not to programs that are adopted as teacher-proof plans
that claim success for every child but are, in reality, effective for few.

Teachers like Karen should be viewed as assets, not threats, to the development of responsive and thoughtful curriculum. They should not feel the
need to be compliant. Indeed, brave districts should support noncompliance
with the "mutual respect" that is "necessary for a healthy democracy."

Demands for compliance lead to a dead end. They feed distrust as
teachers stop trusting decisions made by the district office and by district-
sponsored committees. They force teachers into being complicit in teaching children that school is not a place to make meaning or uncover possibilities for learning. Such demands teach teachers to comply, above all

else, to get through a day's work, rather than to see teaching as a joyful way to help others make sense of and contribute to a complex world.

KAREN'S IDENTITY

Karen feels the pain of compliance. It is a pain rooted in her knowledge that her compliance makes her complicit with a program that is not good for all of her students. It is a pain that emanates from scripts that deny the relational nature of teaching. Each day she feels the pain of being an agent for the district office in the delivery of something to her students that is teaching her students that reading is barking sounds, saying nonwords, being compliant, and lacking in joy. This influences Karen's identity as a teacher. She feels herself acting differently and being different from the progressive educator she knows herself to be. She knows that she is becoming different to her students because of the activities in which she has them engage. Her operational definition of herself as a teacher—defining herself in some ways by *what* she does—leaves her hurt.

Little things that Karen does begin to stand metaphorically for other things. She explains:

> I didn't have to order tempera paint or chart paper this year. I was doing the order and didn't need paint or chart paper. Do you know what that means? It means we didn't paint and we didn't put many things on charts this year. There was just no time.

There was no time for Karen's room to reflect who she was, her joy of painting and the pleasure her students typically have when things are printed on and read from charts posted around the room.

Even if her students were to increase by 5% on standardized tests compared with her class of the previous year, she knows that the number is meaningless. Each year the children are different, the social dynamics involved in learning are different, and the needs of the children are different. Scores differ from year to year because of many influences, not one program. Each year is a new story, a new adventure, and very different possibilities and outcomes. Karen and teachers like her accuse tests of not capturing the variety and richness of children's accomplishments. They're right (Altwerger & Bird, 1982). Karen feels the pain of knowing that she cannot address the differences in her students because she is delivering curriculum, not teaching students.

She feels the pain of being complicit, through her actions, in working to create some sort of standardized student who, theoretically, can know everything that every other standardized child knows. Karen knows that such standardized children are a myth rooted in misinterpretations of standards. No sensible standards would suggest that all children could know the same thing in the same way. Karen's pain is in knowing that she defers what she knows and who she is—her identity—in favor of what is mandated.

A teacher who enjoys learning teaches joy (Meyer, 1996), regardless of whether she or he is teaching literacy, Spanish, or physics. A teacher who is curious teaches curiosity. A mean-spirited teacher teaches meanness, blaming, and anger. Karen is a caring and curious teacher. She loves to explore with children as they make sense of their worlds and she makes sense of hers. Although our actions do not define us, Karen's actions and the emotions attached to them have changed her relationship with her students. Her own confusion and dissatisfaction does not detract from her love for her students, but it does frustrate her as she does not have time to pursue children's and her own passions.

I have always had hope in the resilience of children (and now for teachers, too). Yet Karen and I both know that she is a different teacher this year. Rather than being proud of her classroom, recall that she told me that I wouldn't recognize her teaching this year. Her pride has turned to embarrassment. Karen's classroom is still a safe place for children, but her students do not have access to her full teaching repertoire, to all of her talents and skills, to the very essence of who she is, or to the abundance of her teaching identity.

WHAT ARE WE CULTIVATING?

In closing, I return to another work by Maya Angelou (1992), in which she discussed growing things:

> Of course, there is no absolute assurance that those things I plant will always fall upon arable land and will take root and grow, nor can I know if another cultivator did not leave contrary seeds before I arrived. I do know, however, that if I leave little to chance, if I am careful about the kinds of seeds I plant, about their potency and nature, I can, within reason, trust my expectations. (p. 92)

Karen's life work is about growing readers. She imagines children loving books, writing stories, exploring the world, making contributions to the good and addressing the bad, and perpetuating a love of reading. Yet in the cultivation of her garden of readers, she now faces other cultivators who are leaving "contrary seeds" in the minds of children. Karen faces tough decisions as she considers her role in the placing of those seeds; she agonizes about leaving children's reading lives "to chance" when she can not teach from what she understands of her children's literacy lives. She worries, as do I, about the expectations being delivered in the phonics program she enacts daily and fears that her teaching identity is being undermined.

This chapter ends on a less hopeful note, but that is not my ultimate intention in writing this book. There is hope, as you will see. If I did not have hope, I wouldn't be writing.

YOUR THOUGHTS

Now that you have a deeper understanding of Karen's knowledge, you also have insights into how she views children. What is the place of children in the phonics program? How are they receiving the teaching they experience during this time of the day? What are they learning in the immediate and the long term? These are questions to consider as we look more closely at children's lives in the phonics program.

5

A Closer Look at the Children

Acknowledging the complexity of early reading and writing develop-
ment means that we must try to understand literacy from the child's
perspective, and that involves disciplined, systematic observation of
children as they work at reading and writing in and out of classroom
settings.

—Taylor (1993, p. 34)

FROM THE CHILD'S PERSPECTIVE

In this chapter, my focus is on trying to understand children's learning during phonics lessons. Using a variety of analytical perspectives, my purpose
is to make sense of the children's experiences because they ultimately contribute to the children's literacy identities. I admit at the outset of this chapter that more research needs to be done in this area. Unlike many of the publishers of phonics programs, I cannot assert that the program is good for
every child. Nor can I say that the program has long-term negative effects
on the children. Children are quite resilient. I do assert that the behaviors of
the children during the lessons, the fact that scores at lower socioeconomic
status (SES) schools such as Karen's rose minimally, and the district's push
to continue nonproven strategies for teaching contribute to children's reading identities in ways that we must consider.

CHILDREN'S BEHAVIOR
AND WHAT IT SUGGESTS

Let's review some of the behaviors in which the children engaged during
the phonics lesson:

1. One child has carefully rolled up one leg of his jeans and works at unraveling his sock.
2. A few of the children are rocking back and forth.
3. One child is quietly making the sounds of bombs dropping ("eeeyowwwwwww plichhhh").
4. One of the children picks his nose; eventually others do this, too.
5. A child plays with her ears.
6. A child is rubbing her hands up and down her braids (later she'll undo and redo them).
7. One child is poking (in a friendly manner) another.
8. One child is pulling at the rug.
9. Children chat with friends.
10. A child sucks his bracelet.
11. A child is styling her cuticles with her thumbnail.

There are a variety of ways to make sense of the children's behaviors. One explanation is that the children were engaged in self-stimulating behaviors often identified in children with emotional and behavioral problems (R. Udell, personal communication, December 8, 1997). Children want and expect stimulation in school. When that stimulation does not address their broad repertoire of needs for academic or cognitive stimulation, the children seek other forms of stimulation. Simply stated, the children could not gain mental stimulation from the stuff of school at hand so they sought other types of stimulation. They engaged in the soothing behaviors of rocking back and forth or rubbing their ears. Ear rubbing is quite soothing; try it at your next faculty meeting. Sucking behaviors, nose picking, self-grooming activities, and reaching out to touch another are all ways that children (and sometimes adults) seek stimulation. The intention of self-stimulation is some sort of pleasure—in this case, a physical comfort.

Children want and expect school to be stimulating. They might not be able to state this in a lofty articulate fashion, but they may boldly call out, "This is boring," especially in the younger grades. Karen's children had already passed through the "this is boring" stage because it was October when I visited. They were used to the routine of the classroom. Just like their teacher, they acquiesced. They had to in order to survive and to get to better parts of the day. In chapter 2, I discussed the three categories of children's responses to the phonics lesson: (a) the "we get it gang"; (b) those involved in "procedural display participation"; and (c) random responses (including silence). What fascinates me is that all of the children engaged in the behaviors bulleted earlier. There was no consistent pattern of which group acted in these typically socially unacceptable ways during the lesson. This suggests that there were many children frustrated by the intense block of time devoted to the lesson and by the oftentimes meaningless content. I offer as evidence of the last statement the radical change in behaviors when Karen took out the library book about dinosaurs and read that.

IT'S MORE THAN SELF-STIMULATION

When considered as self-stimulating behaviors, our understanding of the children's responses to the phonics lessons is focused *within* the child. A more social view of their behaviors involves paying attention to what their behavior is intended to communicate (communicative intent) to their teacher and colleagues. Snell and Brown (2000) suggested that, "Many problem behaviors are attributed to specific pragmatic intents; that is, the behavior serves a specific function for the individual and is a form of communicating for the individual" (p. 101).

Within the context of the phonics lesson, the communicative intent of the children is something about which we hypothesize by looking at what the children's behavior expresses or asserts. Communicative intent means that behavior functions to relate with and to others because behavior is social. Those advancing this interpretation of behavior (Durand, 1990) submit that behaviors that might appear to be self-stimulating might better be interpreted as communicating messages to others.

Okay, this is getting thick. But it's important! Hang in there. What I'm saying here is that when we act within a social setting, our actions have intentions because we want something, want to do something, or want something to happen in our relationships with others. Because we want something, our behavior has functions. For example, when I see my friend, I might smile at him and wave. My intention is to say hello and let him know we're connected by friendship. My behavior functions to show my intentions. If you were watching only me, you might think it strange that I walk around smiling and waving. Yet if you look in the broader social setting, you see my friend and interpret my actions differently.

Durand (1990) offered four functions for communicative intent. A child might want social attention, might want to demonstrate that he or she is escaping, might want some sort of consequence, or might want some sort of sensory stimulation with another person. All of these functions were present during the phonics lesson. The children touched each other and spoke out to gain social attention. They announced their escape from the lesson by assuming other endeavors such as picking their noses or picking at the carpet. They wanted teacher attention (a consequence) by orally demanding meaning from nonwords. Their touching of each other resulted in sensory stimulation from others (touching back).

The communicative intent for some children was to say, "I quit this lesson. I quit this phonics stuff." Sucking on a bracelet is one way of making such an announcement. For others, it was, "I'm angry, feel hurt, and want you to know that. I won't hurt others but I will hurt my clothing." Still, for others, the communicative intent (the message to others) was that, "There is no joy in the lesson, but there is joy and even discovery in picking my nose." The use of communicative intent to explain behavior acknowledges the social setting in which learning is to take place. The literature on communicative intent is part of the special education literature, yet it applies here.

A concern about communicative intent is that a teacher that views the phonics curriculum as the way to teach reading might suggest that some of her children are behaviorally disordered because they do not behave during phonics. Such teachers might refer their students for testing because of their concern. This exemplifies the social construction of a learning disability (Richardson, Casanova, Placier, & Guilfoyle, 1989) and occurs when the curriculum takes precedence over the children's needs.

WHY CAN'T THE CHILDREN BEHAVE?

Some readers might be wondering why Karen did not simply tell the children to behave during the phonics lesson. Readers might think that she cannot control her classroom. But Karen can control her classroom. She typically relies on the children's understanding of the events in which they are participating as leading to acceptable behaviors. During writers' workshop, the children understand what they are supposed to do, and it makes sense to them. They might write letters, stories, poems, and so on, but during phonics, understanding wanes as the children experience language in a way that does not make sense to many of them. The differences between activities that make sense and those that don't have a profound effect on children's behavior and issues of classroom management. The differences in behavior can be explained using Diaz, Neal, and Amaya-Williams'

(1990) discussion of the differences between self-control and self-regulation. Self-control is a "response to internalized command[s] . . . organized in rigid stimulus response connections [and relies on] environmental cues [to] serve as stimuli for behavioral responses" (p. 130). Self-regulation is "guided according to self-formatted plan[s] . . . changed . . . according to changing goals and situations . . . [and] uses aspects of the environment as tools and mediators to attain goals" (p. 130).

The phonics lesson is about self-control because so many of the children must sit through meaninglessness. We need to teach children to behave, of course, but for what purposes and to what ends? They may need to learn to sit quietly at a concert, but a concert has meanings as well as rules for behavior. The *goals* and *plans* of other times of the day in Karen's room and the *functional systems* of times such as writers' workshop also have meanings—they are environments for growth as a literate soul. They are successful because of the children's self-regulation.

The ambivalence that Karen feels comes from having seen her students behave when they are engaged in something that is appropriate and challenging for them. For example, writing is not an easy process, as any writer knows, but it's one that allows each child to express him or herself at a rate, pace, and intensity that is appropriate for them. Karen makes decisions about what they might learn next, using what she understands about written language development.

The short answer is, yes, she could **make** them sit politely. However, Karen knows that an overreliance on demanding self-control has a high price for a teacher. She knows that if she asks them to or demands that they engage in nonsense on a daily basis that she will lose credibility with them. She knows that to demand self-control for a full hour of nonsense will result in a fundamental distrust of the teacher as a source of authentic and genuine literacy learning and sacrifices the self-regulation she's working to help her students construct. So Karen tolerates departures from her typical level of expectations of behavior and engagement during phonics.

STILL ANOTHER WAY TO ANALYZE CHILDREN'S BEHAVIOR

Halliday and Hasan (1989) offered another way to explain what happened during the phonics lesson. Halliday and Hasan used three terms to help us understand the ways in which a text (meaning a written text or the text of a conversation or, in this case, a teaching situation) may be analyzed and understood. The terms are *field*, *tenor*, and *mode*. Here's how they explained them:

> The field . . . refers to what is happening, to the nature of the social action that is taking place: what is it that the participants are engaged in, in which the language figures as some essential component?
>
> The tenor . . . refers to who is taking part, to the nature of the participants, their statuses, and roles: what kinds of role relationship obtain among the participants, including permanent and temporary relationships of one kind or another, both the types of speech role that they are taking on in the dialogue and the whole cluster of socially significant relationships in which they are involved?
>
> The mode . . . refers to what part the language is playing, what it is that the participants are expecting the language to do for them in that situation: the symbolic organization of the text, the status that it has, and its function in the context, including the channel (is it spoken or written or some combination of the two?). (p. 12)

FIELD, TENOR, AND MODE DURING PHONICS

There are significant differences in field, tenor, and mode between the scripted parts of the phonics lesson and during the reading of the dinosaur library book by Karen. I present this analysis within the phonics lesson first.

The Field of the Phonics Lesson

Field addresses the question "What is happening?" (Halliday & Hasan, 1987, p. 12) in a social sense during a language event. Remember, my focus here is the children. The "nature of the social action" is complicated. Children are rolling around, picking noses, and so on, and do not seem to be engaged (Cambourne, 1995) in the lesson. The role that language plays is a sort of glue that keeps the children at the rug, but for many of the children there is little social interaction beyond that of being present and in the group. The meaning of the language stuff at hand does not bind them together or engage them. Rather, the essential component of language is the script that dictates what is said and controls the use of time. The children are doing what they can to get through the lesson as their teacher reads it.

In some ways, this is a power situation. The children are being told by their teacher, whom they love, to sit through phonics. They acquiesce out of love, respect, or the goal of finishing the lesson. Daily, it becomes clear that real books and their own writing is more important to their teacher, but they must endure phonics to get to authentic (Wortman, 1991) reading and writing.

The setting is reminiscent of times when my mother dragged me to a Sunday school faculty meeting after Sunday school and I sat quietly, well behaved, while folks talked of things and my consciousness of their conversation drifted in and out as I found more interesting things to think about: the colors of their shoes, the colors of their hair, the vent in the ceiling, the discussion of Bobby who was not attending regularly, the growling of my stomach, and so on. I behaved because my mother expected it and because my presence was as a guest who needed to wait for a ride home. Someone else's language agenda kept me present. Had I been expected to participate, I probably would have engaged as the children in Karen's class did by echoing, calling out things that were not relevant, or being quiet and feeling some of the pressure associated with such a choice.

The Tenor of the Phonics Lesson

I previously discussed the "we get it gang" and the other groups during the phonics lesson. The tenor is interesting during the lesson because it is so different from the rest of Karen's day with the children. During phonics, they sit and remain relatively passive. They are asked to assume the status of empty vessels to be filled. Karen assumes the role of the all-knowing teacher of phonics, vicariously through the scripts she reads. The scripts place her in a position of authority about language—a role she plays out quite differently when she is kidwatching during the rest of her day.

The Mode of the Phonics Lesson

Symbolically, the language activity during the phonics lesson binds the children to the rug, but not to each other. It binds them to saying things that sound like language, but do not make meaning as language should. It binds them to one place, but not a place in which the teacher's definition of reading can be expressed operationally. The text has the status of "all-knowing" as the children are given pieces of language to mimic, manipulate, and dissect. All the decisions about the language activity have been made without the children present, meaning that they are not players in the event as much as they are expected to be puppets in it. Many of them become like Sniggles, waiting for the hand of the publisher or writer of the program to operate their voices.

FIELD, TENOR, AND MODE DURING
THE LIBRARY BOOK READING

Now let's consider the field, tenor, and mode of the reading of the library book about dinosaurs.

The Field of the Library Book Reading

In a social sense, the book becomes a point of origin for much interesting conversation. The children listen to Karen's reading, spontaneously react to the text, react to each other, initiate small side conversations, and listen to more of the text. The book is also the point of origin of social activity, in that we could map each turn at speaking that children take and to whom and what they are responding. We would see that there is a complicated web formed by all these interactions. During the phonics lesson, there is no web. There is a straight line from the teacher's script to the children and from the children to the teacher. The two exceptions to this are when the children demand meaning for a word ("schoolbun") and when they protest the use of "dam" as one of the words they can construct. During the reading of the library book, there is a flurry of social and language activity. The essential role of the book, then, is as a vehicle for bringing background knowledge to the foreground, framing questions about the content of the book, and initiating social interactions around an area of knowledge and experience (dinosaurs).

The Tenor of the Library Book Reading

The children's relationships with each other, their teacher, and text change during the reading of the book. Physically, they move closer to Karen, temporarily stop self-stimulating and other behaviors that indicate a lack of engagement, and feel more comfortable spontaneously volunteering comments (which are relevant to the text at hand). Their relationship with Karen changes as she is no longer involved in using the curriculum that holds them hostage on the rug (yes, I know that *hostage* is a strong word). Instead, the children volunteer ideas that Karen has not considered, respond to each others' thoughts, and reconsider her own wonderings about certain parts of the text. The shift is toward a mutuality in which language is a vehicle for exploring, explaining, challenging, and presenting. Such a context would more effectively support the study of sounds that letters make. While the children are engaged with the text, a good kidwatcher can make decisions about phonetic (and other language) elements to teach the children. Bobbie Fisher (1998), Reggie Routman (1996), Carol Avery (1993), and Joann Hindley (1996) are a few teachers who describe doing this type of engaging work with phonics in their classrooms.

Karen knows that young children develop a deep relationship with their teacher when they are respected, cared for, and loved (Goldstein, 1998, 1999). If she works on making them behave "like little angels" during phonics, she risks undermining their learning at other important times of the day. Notice that they have learned to stay in the rug area and to display some semblance of focus on the lesson. Karen won't ask for more because of the toll it would take on the tenor of her relationships with her children.

The Mode of the Library Book Reading

Mode addresses "what part the language is playing" in a language event. During the reading of the story, the children's expectations turn to language as meaning-based and meaning-making. The children's move in to be closer to each other, the text, and their teacher is a metaphor for the part language is playing. The book signifies unification of purpose: We all want to be included and we all **can** be included. The child just learning English is valued as well as the precocious reader; each voice becomes significant because it may stir an idea or reaction by a colleague. It becomes important to listen to each other because one participant's contributions serve as a doorway for another's thinking and entry into the conversation. Each child's expertise, curiosity, and questioning are intimately tied to the text at hand.

Does that sound too romantic? I argue that it's not because the children shed their self-stimulating behaviors, move closer, strain to see and hear, and present very different communicative intents during the reading of the library book. The library book is one that the children will want to read on their own, with friends, and perhaps borrow to read with their families. The book was an oasis of sorts because during the dry trek through the phonics lesson children initiated certain behaviors to survive. The book served as a reminder of a deeper humanity and of legitimate purposes of text by welcoming a variety of voices, multiples responses, and a change in the role of the teacher from transmitter to partner.

TWO CLASSROOMS IN ONE

Understanding classroom events through field, tenor, and mode helps explain why we see very different children at different times of the school day. Karen's classroom was two different classrooms. Both of the classrooms made assumptions about children, learning, the use and place of language, and the role of relationships in learning. One classroom, the one that was enacted during phonics, ignored the specific children at hand, their interests, their skills, and their knowledge. That classroom was the puppet of the phonics program. The other classroom had a professional teacher who made decisions reflective of the children before her. Karen and her students lived each day in both of these classrooms.

During some parts of the school day, the children put aside one view of themselves and their teacher. During that time, they do phonics. At other times during the day, that view is available and active. What does all this mean for Karen's students as readers? This takes us back to the definition of reading . . . this time, from the children's point of view.

WHAT IS READING
FOR KAREN'S STUDENTS?

In previous chapters, I discussed the definitions of reading among researchers, myself, and Karen. The children in Karen's class are learning what reading is as well. Consider the text that the children were exposed to during the lesson, in particular the story about the cat who took a nap on the (mouse) pad (for a computer), in the pan, in a hat, and in a cap. This story teaches more than the behavior of a cat. It teaches the publisher's definition of reading that may get passed on to the children.

The publishers of the program explain that these little books are needed because they are decodable books. A decodable book, as operationally defined by the publisher, has in it words that can be made from the sounds the children have studied in isolation and in words (both real and non-words) during phonics lessons. Some of the words in the little books are referred to as "jail words," "slippery words," "tricky words," and so on by publishers. These are words that are labeled as not phonetically regular and are to be taught as sight words (words the children must memorize). The word "some" is an example of such a word because the silent <e> does not make the <o> long.

But there's a problem. As Yetta Goodman (1999) suggested, decodable books are not decodable. They are not decodable because the letter–sound system in English is not reliable (see Appendix). More important, if you understand that decoding involves getting the message or meaning (a code is not decoded until you get meaning), a book with "simple" decodable words is even more problematic. If the book says that "*the cat had sat at that pad and pan and had a hat,*" it teaches that reading is the saying of a string of words, not getting meaning. Decodable books are not "simple" because they demand that the child stretch from supposedly regular words and sounds to meaning. That's too big of a stretch in the cat story.

Yetta Goodman (1999) also argued that such books are not predictable, either, although the publishers suggest otherwise as they call the books predictable and decodable. With a strong focus on having the sounds be "regular" (and they are not), the books lose sense. Without sense, they are not predictable. By forcing the cat to take a nap on a mat, children are asked to focus on a welcome mat. How many know what one is? How many know that a mouse pad can be abbreviated to simply be referred to as a pad? (I didn't know this.) The constrained use of language makes the text unpredictable. It makes it more difficult for children to read, as other researchers have pointed out (Flurkey, 1997; F. Smith, 1985).

Some of the children in Karen's class have a definition of reading as meaning-making. These are the ones who demand to know what nonwords mean and who will make up definitions for them when Karen offers none. With words like "reced," we are stuck, and the children tune them out and move on to the next word, seeking meaning. While the precocious readers may seek meaning, the struggling readers, the English as a second language (ESL) readers, and emerging readers are learning that a lot of nonsense gets said when we are dealing with words. They begin to see words, rather than the making of meaning, as the substance of reading. So, in their own reading, what will they do when they come to a word that they have not seen in print before? Researchers like Martens, Goodman, and Flurkey (1995) find that children who have received demonstrations that reading is calling nonwords will call nonwords when they come to words they haven't seen previously in print. They sacrifice meaning in order to say anything—be it a real or nonword—and move on. We know they are sacrificing meaning because they say a word that sounds like (or even looks like) the word in print, but it is not a word that makes sense. Indeed, it might not even be a real word at all. Why should it be? Their teacher had them read nonwords. It's what's to be expected in this stuff called reading.

THEY MUST BE LEARNING SOMETHING

They are.

They Are Learning to Overrely on Phonics

Some of the children are learning about letter–sound relationships. These children are learning to overrely on the phonics cueing system. Most of them are learning to compromise the real reason for reading. Their over-reliance on letter–sound relationships gets in the way of predicting what is coming in a text because they are not constructing meaning as they read. The do not rely on the semantic and syntactic cueing systems because these have been sacrificed to the focus on phonics. Readers should use phonics; they should use it to contribute to the construction of meaning.

They Are Learning a Limiting Definition of Reading

By spending a full hour each day on sounds, the children are learning a very limiting definition of what reading is, what it can be used for, or how to find and celebrate the joys it affords. They are learning that reading is a strange and strained relationship with text, which may bare meaning and may not. They are learning that reading is vague, unpredictable, and unreliable.

The children are each constructing a definition that will be enacted each time they engage with a text. As we study these young readers in the future, we'll learn about their attitudes toward reading, their passion for it, and the uses they put it to. That type of long-range study is begging to be done. Will the publishers of the phonics program do this research? Or will they continue to publish newer and better versions of a program without studying the definition of reading that it teaches young children?

They Are Learning to Comply

Like their teacher, the students are learning to comply. They are learning
that there are times during school—and during life—when we sit quietly
and don't necessarily understand what is going on or what we are supposed to learn. They are learning, in many classrooms that take such programs quite seriously and demand children's "attention," that when they
are told to sit and listen, that is exactly what they should do. They should
sit and listen. Don't think too much. Just demonstrate the appropriate behaviors. Don't ask questions, just follow orders. This is in sharp contrast to
what Karen's students have historically lived in her classroom.

But those days are gone. They are gone, even though the children's
reading and writing portfolios in years gone by demonstrate huge amounts
of growth. They are gone although Karen documented that the children
were learning, thinking, making decisions, and accessing information. The
full hour (or more) in which the underlying lesson is compliance is powerful. It confuses children's understanding of what school is for. School
should be a trustworthy place in which children can make sense of the
world. In Karen's classroom, the compliance that is requested is gentle because of Karen's own sensitivity to what she is an agent for when the class
has phonics each day. Karen understands that what is at stake is greater
than the sounds of letters. Each of her students' identities as readers is in
an ongoing formative process, and those identities are influenced by every
activity she undertakes with them.

THE CHILDREN'S READING IDENTITIES

A reading identity is what reading is in one's life. It is views, attitudes,
uses, beliefs, joys, and sorrows of our reading lives. We all have identities
as readers. We might love reading, use it as a tool, read because we want to
talk with friends about books, read to get ahead in the world (Houle,
1961), or read to find solace and spirit. Some of us hate to read. Where we
stand in terms of reading, our view of it, our relation to the texts, and situations in which we've read or will read all contribute to our reading identities. These identities are the very stuff of our humanity, as Sloan (1991)
suggested:

> The one story is the quest of the human imagination for identity. The frame-
> work of all literature is a myth or archetypal story that goes like this: Once

people lived in a paradisal garden or golden age in harmony with nature. They lost their perfect home, became alienated from nature and each other, and subject to time and death. The metaphorical quest to recover the lost golden age—identity, wholeness, unity—is the framework of all literature. This imaginative quest ranges from the height of our dreams—what we most desire—to the depths of our nightmares—what we most fear and dread.

In supplying us with a vision of imaginative possibilities, literature contributes to our personal visions of the truly human and humane society. (p. 36)

You might wonder what this has to do with children learning to read. If this is the case, I wish you could have visited Karen's classroom before the phonics program was mandated. Or visit some other teacher of young children who knows how to reach into their hearts with books, impassion them with the joy of reading, and entice them to love books and want to join the literacy club (F. Smith, 1988). Teachers like Karen know how to teach phonics while respecting children's call to stories (R. Coles, 1989). They know that the basics begin at imagination, humanity, decency, respect of individuality, and the passions of the child, including their passion to understand and use written language.

Children and adults with healthy brains and developing minds develop reading identities. We all know who "the readers" in our families are. We know the students that arrived at school reading quite well. We know those, including some teachers and family members, that learned to hate to read. They are the ones who tell children to "sound it out" in a whining voice that grates the emerging reader's identity into shreds. Good readers use phonics. They learn to read using phonics *and* the other cueing systems (K. Goodman, 1996). But they learn, above all else, that they are readers who rely on texts as meaningful, joyful, and informative. They relish Sunday mornings with coffee and the newspaper; they read to learn new skills; they read for spiritual enlightenment; they read in bed before they go to sleep; they recall reading under the covers with flashlights; and they remember when something, some event or person, turned them on to reading.

What happens to children who learn that reading is barking out nonwords? What happens to those children whose only chance at reading is in school because home is too busy, too hectic, too poor, too rich, or too chaotic for attention to reading? Like everyone else, their identities are influenced by every event and every interaction with text.

In the devotion to programs like the one Karen must use, we are teaching children that sounds matter more than meaning. As the public, some teach-

ers, and even children begin to "assume that what is tested is what is important" (K. Goodman, Shannon, Freeman, & Murphy, p. 88), the focus will increasingly become sounds, bits of words, and "fractured language" (K.
Goodman, Shannon, Freeman, & Murphy, p. 87). A narrow definition of
reading imposed on our children will not promote a love of reading. A love
of reading goes hand in hand with a love of thinking. We have much at stake
when the reading identities of children are at risk. When their reading identities are reduced to compliant callers of sounds, the best we can hope for is
that school seems ludicrous and they learn elsewhere. The more dismal possibilities include choosing not to learn, choosing not to think, and choosing
not to participate in our democracy.

YOUR THOUGHTS

It is in the spirit of reading identities that we must consider the consequences of curriculum. Johnston's (1998) recent call for a consideration of
the consequential validity of testing, in which he suggested ways in which
tests have consequences that hurt children, can be extended to the call for
studies of the consequential validity of phonics programs. Such studies
should consider the ways in which phonics programs influence children's
reading identities.

The consideration of the phonics mandate as an issue of curriculum is
discussed in chapter 6. What's your view of curriculum? Where should it
come from? Who should make decisions about it? Is it something that can
be delivered or does it construct itself?

6

Phonics Programs
and Curriculum

As soon as students realize that their lessons are about their *meanings, then the entire psychological content of schools is different. Learning is no longer a context between them and something outside of them, whether the problem be a poem, a historical conclusion, a scientific theory, or anything else. . . . In short, the meaning-maker metaphor puts the student at the center of the learning process. It makes both possible and acceptable a plurality of meanings, for the environment does not exist only to impose standardized meanings but rather to help students improve their unique meaning-making capabilities.*
—Postman and Weingartner (1969, p. 97)

WHAT IS CURRICULUM?

I'll define **curriculum** simply. Let's call it *what children experience in school*. In the case of the phonics program, the curriculum came from publishers who made a sale to the district. Those publishers provided inservice programs for the teachers, produced materials, and delivered those materials to the children via the teacher. The curriculum came from far away. It came from a publisher that made generalizations about how the children in Karen's classroom should spend their time. The publisher's view of curriculum is one that views the child as empty, the curriculum as the stuff of what must be put into the child, and the teacher as the conduit that delivers the material from the publisher to the child. It is a view of curriculum that circumvents teacher thinking, child thinking, and unique classroom experiences as integral parts of learning to read.

77

Dewey (1938) discussed curriculum as something that needs to develop locally, even as locally as the classroom, so that teachers and students have input:

> The plan, in other words, is a cooperative enterprise, not a dictation . . . not a mold for a cast-iron result but is a starting point to be developed into a plan through contributions from the experience of all engaged in the learning process. . . . The essential point is that the purpose grows and takes shape through the process of social intelligence. (p. 72)

Dewey's view of curriculum is not available to Karen or her students when a view of curriculum is adopted within a mandated program. They were subjected to a curriculum that was put in place in response to a manufactured crisis (Berliner & Biddle, 1995) at the national, state, and local levels. In Karen's situation, the "plan" *could* have been "cooperative." In the past, it was. The plan *could* have included the "social intelligence" about reading with which Karen's children arrive at school. In the past, it was.

Perrone's (1991) view of curriculum resonates with Dewey's; they both argued that curriculum originates as collective efforts, passions, and interests of all those involved. Perrone wrote:

> We have too much prescription already, and we have engaged in too little thought about the pedagogical implications associated with curriculum decisions. While the curriculum needs some order, it needn't be as tightly drawn as it has become and it should never leave teachers out of what has to be a central decision-making role. (p. 24)

I would add that we cannot leave children out of the decision-making role either. This is something that Karen already knows.

Karen knows how to support children in constructing their worlds as readers. Her reading curriculum has typically come from her knowledge, informed by many experts she's read and heard, and her experiences. Her reading curriculum has typically come from her understanding of the unique language abilities that her students bring to her classroom. This year and in the years since (as the district convinces itself and the public that the phonics program has saved them from eternal illiteracy), Karen's curriculum does not come from her expertise. It comes from a program whose effectiveness has not been proved (G. Coles, 2000; Taylor, 1998).

CURRICULUM AND IDEOLOGY

When the idea of curriculum as being operationally defined as *what children experience in school* is held up to the Postman and Weingartner quote at the beginning of this chapter, some questions arise:

1. Where does the curriculum come from?
2. What is the curriculum *supposed* to do?
3. What is the curriculum doing?

The difficulty in addressing these questions is that they are immediately political: They are about the processes by which curriculum decisions (that influence the child, the teacher, and the school) get made, the place of the child, the place of the teacher, and the reasons for schooling. One goal in this chapter is to discuss curriculum and its impact using the three questions listed above.

Prior to responding to the three questions, I want to make it clear that I take an ideological stance in this chapter. The thesaurus in my computer uses these words as synonyms for **ideology**: beliefs, doctrines, dogma, convictions, strong belief, philosophy, tenets, political idea, and opinions. That's quite a range! The view of curriculum in the chapter is ideological because it is rooted in **my** beliefs about curriculum. The view is ideological because it reflects my convictions, beliefs, and philosophy about the experiences that occur in school (curriculum) that influence learning to read. The ideology presented is based on research about the teaching and learning of reading, my experiences as a teacher of young children for almost 20 years, and my work with preservice and inservice teachers and their students. The ideology is one based on questioning things the way they are with a focus on who has power, how they use that power, who gains by the use of power, and who suffers because of it.

My ideology also comes from progressive views of education and from the perspective that Shannon (1995) called "critical literacy." Critical views of curriculum examine the uses of power; progressive views consider the nature of experience (Dewey, 1938) in the educative process. I hesitate to use the word dogma when discussing ideology because that word suggests an almost blind adherence to beliefs. My beliefs are open to scrutiny and are constantly being enhanced by reading, writing, thinking, experiences, and research.

I include this discussion of ideology to encourage you to think about where your beliefs about curriculum come from. How flexible are those beliefs? Who or what has influenced them? When have they changed? If they have changed, why did they? When you discuss curriculum with others or when you read about the phonics curriculum that Karen is required to follow, what ideological roots can you find that influence your thinking? In terms of critical literacy, who gains from your thinking? Who might not gain? It is in the realization that all thinking about curriculum is ideological that issues of curriculum overflow into politics. It is for that reason that I present some political-curriculum connections in this chapter. I elaborate on them in chapter 8.

WHERE DOES THE CURRICULUM COME FROM?

In the beginning sections of this chapter, I presented my view of curriculum. How would **you** define curriculum? Is curriculum a set of activities that one must do as a teacher and experience as a student? Just how *set* is the set of activities supposed to be?

Recently, Karen explained curriculum as a response to tests. Her district, worried about reading test scores, adopted a curriculum that is supposed to address reading weaknesses in the district and result in higher test scores. In this situation, curriculum comes from test score worries. (Interestingly, some of the companies that write and publish the tests also sell products to increase test scores as well as curriculum packages that claim to do the same thing.) Madaus (1999) explained how a view of curriculum being driven by tests is wrong-headed:

> What is needed at this juncture in American education is more discussion of creative counterstrategies that have curriculum and instruction driving testing rather than testing driving curriculum and instruction–counterstrategies in which testing is the servant not the master of curriculum, instruction, and learning. (p. 107)

Madaus assumes that testing captures and accurately presents what happens in a classroom. Karen's successful use of portfolios (Graves & Sunstein, 1993) with her young students provides a more in-depth and sustained way that progress can be presented. Her students' portfolios are thinner than usual this year because there's less time to read, respond to reading, and write. The situation in Karen's classroom is the result of standardized test scores being published in a way that led the public to believe that the children of the district were failing to learn to read. The ensuing panic is rooted in the public's blind faith in the accuracy of the tests in measuring reading, the reading curriculum, students, teachers, and schools. Blind faith in the tests leads to the search for the ideal prefabricated curriculum that will fix the students' performances on the tests. This means that curriculum comes from faith and trust in publishers—faith and trust that this book is challenging.

WHAT IS THE CURRICULUM *SUPPOSED* TO DO?

Each of us needs to answer this question for ourselves, as teachers, parents, researchers, community members, politicians, and so on. Each of us must answer the deeper question, too, which is this: What is school for? When we decide what school is for, we can think about curriculum as supporting that. Is curriculum (or school) supposed to perpetuate what already exists? Is it supposed to train individuals to be good workers? Is that the same as educating them to be thoughtful and productive members of our democratic society?

The publishers of the phonics program that Karen uses are not necessarily evil, mean-spirited individuals out to create a society of compliant automatons who will follow any orders given to them. The publishers want children to learn to read, and learning to read with their program will lead to more sales. Publishers are about sales (Ohanian, 1999). The eagerness to make sales should be overshadowed by sound research on the program, but that has not been the case (Allington, 1997; Taylor, 1998). Instead, relying on the national panic about reading scores, publishers move in to districts with strategic plans for convincing teachers (and many others) that the publisher's program can rescue students.

The reading curriculum is supposed to teach the children to read. Some of the children—and Karen can identify which few—might benefit from the phonics program. When curriculum is defined as *what children experience in school*, some of the children are experiencing a learning wasteland. Is that what the curriculum is supposed to do? Is it supposed to waste time? The only way that curriculum cannot waste time is if teachers are permitted to make decisions about children's experiences. Teachers need to be active partners (along with families, researchers, and other district experts) in the cooperative adventure of learning. If teachers have increasingly limited input into decisions about how time in school is spent, they cannot have a significant influence on the children's learning.

WHAT IS THE CURRICULUM DOING?

When the uniqueness of the children is deferred to the prefabricated mandated curriculum, children learn that school ignores who they are. They learn that schools are NOT about standards, but that schools are about some impossible process of standardization. Delivering a standard curriculum to all children teaches them that they are not unique, that their differences do not matter in school, and that their differences and uniqueness will not be cultivated at school. The message of homogeneity that the curriculum delivers is as powerful as the message of the definition of reading that the curriculum delivers. Both messages undermine the uniqueness of teachers, students, schools, and communities, and serve to dismiss the possibilities of teaching and learning that exist as potentials waiting to be realized.

Sadly, we might never know the effects of the phonics program because my guess is that it won't be around long enough to study. Publishers will offer the new and improved version of the program. They will sell parts to enhance certain aspects of the program because test scores don't rise enough, but the newer and improved version will cure that. This is the world of curriculum publishers. It is a fast-paced business world in which things change at the whim of a score on a standardized test or the often-political moves involved in statewide adoptions of reading programs in high-population states. Dewey (1904) was well aware of curriculum rooted in reaction rather than thoughtfulness—almost 100 years ago:

> The tendency of educational development to proceed by reaction from one thing to another, to adopt for one year, or for a term of seven years, this or that new study or method of teaching, and then as abruptly to swing over to some new education gospel, is a result which would be impossible if teachers were adequately moved by their own independent intelligence. The willingness of teachers, especially of those occupying administrative positions, to become submerged in the routine detail of their callings, to expend the bulk of their energy upon forms and rules and regulations, and reports and percentages, is another evidence of the absence of intellectual vitality. (p. 241)

Yet if curriculum is what children experience in school, what is it that the curriculum is doing? We can see that Dewey was concerned about the lack of "intellectual vitality" for teachers in schools. The phonics curriculum is an ongoing experience (an hour of every day for most of the school year) of a lack of intellectual vitality for children (and teachers). When the child who was unraveling his socks left the phonics lesson, he read a book that was in his desk. He was slow to line up for lunch because he wanted to keep reading. His mind, and the minds of many of the children in the class, were searching for an arena that would cultivate their intellectual vitalities. When none was found during the hour of phonics, what was the nature of their experience in school? How would they answer the question "Honey, what did you do in school today?" as their tired family members put them to bed?

What is the curriculum doing? It is contributing to mindlessness for our children. It is detracting from the "having of wonderful ideas" that Duckworth (1987) demanded of schools. It is undermining school as a place of imagination (Greene, 1995) and social action (Shannon, 1995). It is teaching compliance, not respect or self-regulation. It is teaching teachers that they are unprofessional technicians who are to comply by reading scripted lessons.

What is the curriculum doing? It is holding the children and their teacher hostage, preventing them from meaningful and meaning-based learning. It is creating a level playing field in a way that undermines individuality and squelches learning. Remember the child who said he could use the cards to make "candy" if he had a <y>? That child was demonstrating what he knew. Karen, responding to her commitment to try the program, could honor the child's thoughtfulness only in passing. That child was presenting a thoughtful self who was working to legitimize the activity in terms of his own proficiency as a reader. But the program does not allow for this. It is truly "one size fits all" in orientation, and that "all" includes the children and their teacher. It includes all teachers in every district that adopts the program.

What is the curriculum doing? It is telling teachers that children must be taught little bits a little at a time, suggesting that small children have small brains, which should be dealt with as small minds. But children have large minds, rich in ideas, language, and experiences. Children learn to read the names of dinosaurs, planets, and more. Karen knows this. Yet the message is that small minds need lots of different activities compressed into an intense period of time to learn. This was one of the biggest complaints about "Sesame Street" (Healy, 1990), which has since been changed. The awareness that children need time to think and imagine about what they are learning led the producers of that TV show to slow it down, but not the phonics program. The phonics program teaches children that school is a place where things are presented in this fashion: small bits, quick-paced, lacking in meaning, changing focus often, and demanding the isolation of sounds (that can't be isolated). In other words, school is where one learns things that aren't applicable to places besides school. It is a place where you go and learn to respond in nonmeaningful ways.

However, isn't the phonics program teaching children to read? I defer to Richard Allington on that question. Allington (1997), a well-known and respected researcher, stated quite simply, "Show me the research." He pointed out that there is no research to demonstrate the effectiveness of the kind of direct systematic intense phonics programs like the one Karen is forced to use.

IS THIS WHAT WE WANT
FROM CURRICULUM?

In light of my response to the three questions posed earlier, I have to wonder whether we want everything that the phonics curriculum is delivering to Karen's students, to Karen, and to our greater community. We do want children's experiences in school to support and actively contribute to their literacy development. There are ways to teach reading that respond to the needs of many more of the readers in the classroom than the *one size fits all* orientation of the phonics program. As long as teachers bring children from meaningful text to discussions of the parts of words and back to meaningful texts, the basic integrity and substance of reading will be maintained. In Mills and O'Keefe's (1992) book, they explained how to teach phonics in a way that supports reading as meaning-making. Moustafa (1997) offered teachers the idea of using onsets (everything up to the vowel) and rimes (from the vowel on) to study words.

Roller (1996) showed how struggling readers learn to read and learn to love reading when the instruction they experience is based on their strengths and their interests. Roller went so far as to suggest that we stop discussing *disability* in terms of reading and focus instead on *variability*. Children's differences—their uniquenesses—can be the point of origin for curriculum and lead to effective and efficient readers. That's what children need from curriculum. That's what Karen wants from the curriculum in her classroom when she says that the mandate is not for every child.

Teachers and learners are most effective when curriculum is "practical, situated, and personal" (Paris, 1993, p. 78). In other words, when teachers **can** be agents for children's learning rather than agents for publishers, they are increasingly effective. Paris documented teachers' increased sense of ownership of the curriculum and their students' learning when those teachers were supported as thinkers. The shift here is to put the learners' experiences at the center. This does not mean that the children dictate curriculum by saying, for example, that they want to study only dinosaurs. The teacher's expertise does not get discounted when curriculum becomes learner centered. However, all experiences are legitimated. Fox (1993), an author, teacher educator, and reading researcher, put it this way: "*If we allowed children to show us what they could do* they would probably learn a lot faster than we permit them to at present" (p. 66). In other words, the children, with an informed teacher's input, will set standards for themselves far above and far different from what publishers are offering in the phonics program.

It makes little sense to have a curriculum that demands the study of language out of a meaningful context. Whitehead (1949) wrote that,

> The solution which I am urging, is to eradicate the fatal disconnection of subjects which kills the vitality of our modern curriculum. There is only one subject-matter for education, and that is Life in all its manifestations. (p. 18)

Karen knows this all too well when she complains that, "They're taking the life out of my teaching."

LIFE IN ALL ITS MANIFESTATIONS

I stated earlier that curriculum is what children experience in school. It is also what their teachers experience in school. Ultimately, curriculum leads to knowledge that emanates from the experiences that one has had (Wells, 1999). Teachers' and students' experiences and knowledge help them define their worlds. Another of the mandates from the central district office that accompanied the mandate for the use of the phonics program was the demand that all newly hired teachers use the basal reader for the first 3 years of their teaching in the district. Principals were now expected to ensure that newly hired teachers used the phonics program and the basal reading program. The experiences of new teachers are now bound to two specific mandates that prevent teachers from actively making decisions except, perhaps, which children might be in which reading group, if they group their children for reading.

These curricular decisions manifest themselves in the teachers' and students' growing definitions of themselves as readers and learners. These curricular decisions manifest themselves in teachers' increased frustration with a system that will not let them be professionals or (and by far worse) in teachers becoming dependent on basal systems and scripted phonics programs.

A BALANCING ACT

Simply asked, how might a curriculum such as the phonics curriculum manifest itself in *Life*? One manifestation that is claimed by publishers (and others) is that the call for balance will mean **one** curriculum that is suited for all children and be constituted of a fine blend of phonics and other literacy experiences. But "balance" as operationalized by this district is merely a political balancing act in which certain influential parties (newspapers, politicians, and legislators) are appeased. Real balance is an individual, linguistic, psychological, social, cultural, and spiritual affair. It is organic and a responsive process headed by a professional decision maker. Real balance is respectful of the complex social dynamic that is classroom life. Real balance honors the identity of all that are present, their knowledge, their pasts, their presents, and their exceptionalities. Real balance involves goals reflective of the spirits of democracy, decency, morality, and humanity in every part of the school day.

I am not suggesting here that the district is being deliberately mean-spirited about Karen or her children. Nor do I want readers to understand me as saying that the district-level decisions are uninformed. District-level administrators were reading and citing reports on reading such as Adams (1994) and Snow, Burns, and Griffin (1998). Unfortunately, they often presented their reading as the final and ultimate truth, rather than as documents that ignored certain research and are situated in debates about the most effective ways to teach reading (G. Coles, 2000; Taylor, 1998). Some districts claim that their phonics mandates are part of a balanced approach to teaching reading. "Balance" in the case of Karen's district is created by the immense force of the district (including all those who put weight on the district's curriculum decision making) on one side with every primary teacher and student in the district on the other side. This could more accurately be called curriculum bullying than curriculum balancing.

Curriculum decisions reflect larger issues. Cunningham and Fitzgerald (1996) suggested that, "Knowing different epistemological issues and positions forces us collectively to examine the *world views* implicit in reading organizations, journals, research methods, accepted or popular practices and so on . . . " (p. 36; italics added). That's a complicated statement, but it means that there are different views of just what reading is and that those views are expressed in research, curriculum documents, expectations of classroom activity, views of teachers and children, and views of teaching and learning. The *world view* that the district office wants for all in this district is imposed in a top–down manner and dressed up and presented to teachers and the public under the banner of "balance." But balance, if there can be such a thing, must be created at the places where teachers and children are involved in daily interactions. Curriculum, to be truly authentic, must be a local endeavor that balances the knowledge base in reading (from research with real children in real schools) with the children at hand.

WHAT CURRICULUM COULD BE

Curriculum development can be "mind-full" and "wonder-full" (Duckworth, 1987) and an ongoing process that is demanding and life-changing (Meier, 1995) for teachers and students (Meyer et al., 1998). Curriculum, when viewed as *what children (and teachers) experience in school*, has the potential of being the ultimate expression of a teacher's professionalism and an ultimate learning opportunity for the children. This means that teachers and children need curriculum standards that capture, express, and enact the idea that schools are places in which there can be many and varied possibilities. The view of standards that gave birth to the phonics program that Karen is using is both limited and limiting. Standards that limit possibilities lead to curriculum adoptions that ignore students' differences. Perrone (1998) expressed that sentiment this way: "By and large, this standards movement is more about standardization than standards, and it tends in most cases to look right past the students teachers meet day in and day out in their classrooms" (p. 41).

The appropriation of teacher decision making by a phonics program publisher and administrators underscores the idea that curriculum is political activity. It is political because it involves, among other things, oppression. My hope is that you, as a reader, are beginning to see the political contexts of teaching and that you'll want to act on that political milieu in ways suggested later on in this book. (YES! This is a tease to get you energized, encourage you to keep reading, and entice you to define your world view in a way that involves you as an activist.)

Karen's students have little time to read and write. Their access to books, other texts, and so much of what we know children need to learn to read (Holdaway, 1979; McQuillan, 1998) is severely restricted and controlled. This is oppressive and indicative of the "one size fits few" (Ohanian, 1999) nature of curriculum that limits students' growth. The first-grade studies completed more than 30 years ago (Bond & Dykstra, 1967/1997) showed how little time average students actually read in school in tightly controlled programs. Struggling readers' access to texts was even more restricted. Today, young readers spend less in-school time reading when that time is taken up by phonics lessons.

TIME AND IMAGINATION

Time is a key word here. I hope you remember the child who daydreamed during the journal writing break from phonics. Karen knows the importance of daydreaming because she's a reader and a writer. She tells her students that sometimes she just needs to think and dream about the book she is reading or the piece of writing she is composing. She supports her students in doing the same. Children need to know that they can daydream in school. In her study of daydreaming's influence on children's literacy development, Hanson (1992) discussed children's self-described urgent needs to "imaginate" before they write and during and after their reading. The children in her study invented the word *imaginate*:

> According to these children, daydreaming is integral, often a precursor to imagination. Imagination is then viewed as an intermediate step, taken toward production. . . . The profiled children describe the progression from their invisible mind to visible production as a process of spanning both daydreaming and imagination. (p. 237)

Daydreaming takes time. It takes time to generate ideas, get in touch with passion, and craft meaning from what is read or written. But where is the time for children to imaginate when curriculum overshadows identity? There just isn't enough time in the school day to waste it on programs that don't address the unique literacy identities in the classroom.

WE KNOW TOO MUCH

Most readers know that when a new-to-them word is presented in a text, typically one of two things happens. The reader learns that the word is not that important because it is not repeated or explained and he or she can still make sense of the passage. Or the text will teach the word to the reader (Meek, 1988). If a word is used enough in a text, we can usually figure out what it means. This is how we learned to speak—by listening and watching as we construct meaning. It is how we learn from reading. However, that ambiguity-leading-to-meaning process is being undermined by the presentation of words that we can never define. The message of the phonics curriculum is that texts will NOT teach them what words mean. This is a serious and fundamentally flawed manifestation of the phonics program Karen is forced to use.

Quite simply, we know too much about learning and teaching (Shannon, 1990) to perpetuate a curriculum that is this hurtful. Cazden (1988) presented "three features of classroom life—the language of curriculum, the language of control, and the language of personal identity—the tripartite core of all categorizations of language functions" (p. 3). In her discussion, she suggested that the language of curriculum is "the ideational function" (p. 3); in other words, it is language that is in direct relationship to thinking and thought. The language of control involves "the establishment and maintenance of social relationships" (p. 3). The language of personal identity involves "expression of the speaker's identity and attitudes" (p. 3). Every moment of every school day children are learning about their thinking, their relationships with others (including teachers and texts), and their identities. Karen feels the weight and intensity of the tripartite. It is a weight borne of knowing what she knows about curriculum.

This seems like a lot to bear, doesn't it? Well it is. Informed teachers know it. Meier (1997) described how his school year unfolds as a teacher of young children:

> We could be someone we weren't, make ourselves up; we didn't know each other. But salient bits and pieces of our identities were evident from our first moments together. We couldn't hide. As we carried on each day, for 181 days, we learned each other's foibles and strengths. When weaknesses and areas of difficulty rose to the surface and became public . . . I learned what we needed to address the overall issue of individual differences and work as a classroom community to help each other feel accepted . . . the fight, then, is to keep moving toward closeness and connection, and to learn from the little events and scenes with individual children. (pp. 125–126)

Meier knows that curriculum is connection. It involves embracing children with our knowledge of language, child development, language development, and more. Curriculum involves making decisions and asking questions that provide "a sense of purpose and meaning in learning" (Short & Burke, 1991, p. 55).

Simply put, "Kids need access to teachers who can give them what they need" (Darling-Hammond, 2000). This means that children need access to teachers who are trusted to make curricular decisions based on moral, ethical, and informed goals. It means that curriculum is personal and contextual and cannot be left in the hands of those who do not know the children in specific classrooms. It is this specificity of curriculum that Karen is an expert at. It is a shame that her expertise has been pushed aside and the needs of her students generalized and homogenized to the point of being ignored.

YOUR THOUGHTS

Are you getting mad? Good. (If you answered yes.) Have you noticed a missing piece? Have you noticed that I've made little or no reference to socioeconomic status, culture, or ethnicity? Why? What role do these play in the prescribed teaching of the phonics lesson? Think about that as we venture into the importance of diversity in the phonics program.

7

Phonics, Reading, and Culture

Black people are the magical faces at the bottom of society's well. Even the poorest whites, those who must live their lives only a few levels above, gain their self-esteem by gazing down on us. Surely they must know that their deliverance depends on letting down their ropes. Only by working together is escape possible. Over time, many reach out, but most simply watch, mesmerized into maintaining their unspoken commitment to keeping us where we are, at whatever cost to them or to us.

—Bell (1992, p. 243)

DIVERSITY MATTERS

As I begin writing this chapter, I find it striking that it will be the shortest one in the book. It is striking because Karen's classroom is diverse, and she celebrates that diversity in respectful and relevant ways that go deep into the "well" that Bell mentions. Karen's work, as she sees it, is about "letting down ropes." She has explored issues of racism, gender, and equity with her young students in a variety of ways that I do not present here. I do not present those here because this book is about a phonics program's influence. In case you haven't noticed, I have mentioned only superficial descriptions of Karen's children, beyond their behavior. That is because, during the teaching of phonics, issues of difference are erased and ignored by the phonics program. This is a program that the publishers' consultants, when they visit the district, tell teachers "is good for all children." The quest for homogeneity of curriculum and the systematic dismissal of children's and teachers' identities may seem efficient for the delivering of cur-

91

riculum. These are strategies that also can be interpreted as lacking in sensitivity to cultural differences.

I am not suggesting that the publishers of the phonics program are racists, committed to maintaining an unfair distribution of wealth in our country. I say that their lack of attention to differences can be interpreted as institutionally racist. The presentation of a curriculum that is, on the *surface*, void of color, ethnicity, gender, and culture may seem quite "safe" if the publishers are concerned about seeming racist, which is common in our age of political correctness. Getting below the surface is important because it means not "keeping us where we are" when the *us* is not only the faces at the bottom of the well, but the faces of teachers looking at those faces in the well. It is the faces of teachers who understand how programs—how anything that occurs in schools—is involved in positioning students' cultures as highly prestigious, not having much prestige, or being completely dismissed.

Raising standards and the impact that standards have on members of diverse groups are growing concerns. For example, in Texas, where standards are being raised and phonics programs like the one Karen uses are being instituted, White students have less than a 70% chance of graduating from high school. Black and Latino students have less than a 50% chance of graduating from high school. In reporting on the work of the National Commission on Teaching and America's Future, Darling-Hammond (2000) explained that 49% of the variability of student achievement can be explained by issues having to do with family, such as income and family level of education; 43% of variability in student achievement has to do with teacher qualification as measured by licensing exams and teacher level of education. Scripted programs do not allow for teacher variability. The programs do not address specific needs of specific learners in classrooms. Instead, they offer one script. In the case of Karen, her expertise in dealing with diverse students is dismissed. The pedagogy in the phonics program is culturally insensitive because it is bleached to the point of seeming to have no color.

O'Loughlin and Barnes (1999) presented some disturbing data, reporting that, "Regrettably, schools are not always safe havens where children can construct positive race identifications. To the contrary, some schools are breeding grounds for bigotry" (p. 4). Just as Bell discussed at the beginning of this chapter, O'Loughlin and Barnes went on to state that, "it is still eminently rational for people at the top of the racial status chain to hold onto such beliefs [racism] because the colonial order that created the doctrine of 'natural' inferiority in the first place did so to benefit the dominant social order" (p. 21). This means that a child's identity is always present and being influenced, and that as teachers and researchers we are obligated to always be cognizant of our beliefs, feelings, thoughts, and actions as they saturate our classrooms and research forums. It means that the many cultures in a classroom matter every moment of the school day.

TEACHING DENIED

Karen was not allowed to engage in culturally relevant teaching (Ladson-Billings, 1994) during phonics lessons because she was not afforded the opportunity to develop lessons that reflected the specificity of cultures and ethnicities in her classroom and the broader community. Karen's and the children's cultures were marginalized from school experiences during the entire phonics lesson. The texts to which they can relate and their ways of discussing those texts were shelved. The rest of the day is not exclusive in this way, yet the use of significant classroom time for disenfranchising children sends the message that reading (or phonics, as Karen would label it) exists in a realm that factors out differences. That's just not possible.

Participant structures (Philips, 1971) are the cultural rules that one learns, typically at home and in one's community, for taking part in speaking events. Children come to school with different understandings for when to speak, how to share their words and worlds, and how to use language in their learning. Karen's sensitivity to these issues is part of her teaching that she is proud of. She expects ESL students to learn in fairly predictable ways, yet is open to other ways they have with words. She is sensitive to differences between African-American and Native-American learners because of her work at understanding their cultures. She knows that families have different structures of participation, too.

Karen works at understanding what it means to be a middle-class, middle-aged White woman teaching the children in her class. In other words, her teaching is rooted in identities that come from family life, cultural life, and other facets of living and learning in a diverse society. But all that is placed aside during phonics. It remains present during math, other reading times, science, social studies, music, and other disciplines that her students undertake. But for an hour a day (or more), culture is placed aside. Culture doesn't count. It is forced into the positions of invisibility and silence at the bottom of the well.

Children from the dominant culture succeed in school because of the strong ties between the nature of school and the nature of home. The use of language, "ways with words," is different across cultures, yet schools tend to grow from and cultivate the dominant culture's ways with words. When this is perpetuated, success in reading in school becomes available to fewer children from diverse groups (Heath, 1983). When a competent and successful teacher, having taught many children to read, is condemned to scripted lessons, her teaching is denied, her efficacy is bracketed, and her students' cultures are put on hold.

~~CROSSING OUT CULTURALLY RELEVANT PEDAGOGY~~

Culturally relevant pedagogy means the teacher views herself as an "artist" (Ladson-Billings, 1994, p. 42), has high expectations for all students (p. 44), helps "students make connections between their community, national, and global identities (p. 49), and views her students as sources of knowledge (p. 52) to be valued in school. Culturally relevant pedagogy is teaching that respects and reflects the funds of knowledge (Moll, Veles-Ibanez, & Greenberg, 1990) that a community has and the ways in which a child brings the richness of those funds to school. Karen knows how to teach this way—a way that is based in research. But as Taylor (1998) suggested, important research gets ~~crossed out~~, in this case the importance of culturally relevant pedagogy, when it is dismissed by mandated programs.

Understanding cultural relevance in teaching means understanding one's own position in a diverse society. It means understanding what it means to come from a privileged position. In this case, a privileged position is one that makes going to school seem quite natural, with little difference between the language and culture of home and school. Two well-known writers have captured the feeling of coming from other-than-dominant cultures and trying to live or be within the dominant culture.

In Byrd Baylor's (1992) book *Yes is Better Than No*, she presented this scenario:

> On the reservation you grew up seeing the little rock shelters high in the ledges of the mountains where your ancestors chased out foxes and coyotes and mountain lions to make their own hard sleeping places. You saw where the smoke from their fires had blackened the rocks overhead. You found the ashes of those fires still in the sand and the tiny bones of their rabbit stews still glistening in the sun.
>
> Out there, walking the same rocky land, you live so close to your ancestors that their lives never seem far away from you. Even their way of living

in the caves and the cliffs seems natural enough. You couldn't mind so much living like that. As good as an alley in town anyway.

But of course here in town with the Anglos you have to think in a different way. In their way.

Maria is trying to do that now . . . to think in a different way. In their way. "But I still got me an Indian mind," she says. "It won't think White. It thinks Indian."

"Mine too," Rose says. "That's our trouble." (p. 123)

It is their trouble. It is their trouble if they walk into a classroom that only thinks White. It is their trouble if their teacher expects them to think White. It is their trouble if they are subjected to programs that deny or dismiss the relevance of culture to teaching and learning.

Another example is from Katherine Paterson's (1981) autobiographical look at reading and writing children's books. She described the point in her childhood when she moved from the United States to Japan for 4 years and all the struggles she had in learning a new language and a new culture without her family present. On returning to the United States, she finds that she has changed.

In 1961, after four years in Japan, I boarded a jet in Tokyo and landed about twenty hours later in Baltimore. I was met by my parents and one of my sisters and taken home to Virginia. Every night for many weeks I would get out of the soft bed, which was killing my back, and lie sleepless on the floor. I was utterly miserable. "These people," I would say to myself, meaning my own family, "these people don't even know me." The reason I thought my family didn't know me was that they didn't know me in Japanese.

You see, in those four years I had become a different person. I had not only learned new ways to express myself, I had new thoughts to express. I had come by painful experience to a conclusion that linguists now advance: *language is not simply the instrument by which we communicate thought. The language we speak will shape the thoughts and feelings themselves.* (pp. 7–8; italics added)

Katherine could not explain her pain to others until she was older and had read what linguists say about the connection among language, culture, and learning. As a student in school, she would have relied on her teachers to have that understanding. The scripted curriculum dismisses the teacher's knowledge and relegates the students' cultures to outside of the classroom walls. Culture is made to seem irrelevant, but it's not.

GETTING UNCOMFORTABLE

The main point I want to make in this chapter is about culture and the importance of understanding that culture influences every context to which we come. Applebee (1996) discussed knowledge-out-of-context as knowledge that is devoid of conversation—knowledge that may be memorized but is not useful because it is "stripped of the contexts that give it meaning" (p. 3). Knowledge-in-action is knowledge that is contextualized, seen as useful and engaging, and has a greater chance of becoming part of our long-term memories and being of subsequent use in new and different situations.

Phonics can be taught either way. Karen used to teach it in-action, using familiar rhymes, songs, raps, and more. She knew she was teaching a diverse group of children and responded by addressing skills they would need (Delpit, 1995) in ways that made sense to them. Now her teaching is reduced to an out-of-context setting and may be quite void of meaning for many of her children. Our cultural links are what support us in bringing meaning to a language event. The joys of exploring and learning language in-action are deprived of too many in the scripted lessons of the phonics program.

Macedo (2000) said this quite eloquently when he wrote that, "What needs to be understood is that educators can not isolate phoneme-grapheme awareness from social class and cultural identity factors . . ." (p. 19). He went on to say that these "factors" contribute to our identities and our views on and ultimate actions in the world. This means stretching ourselves as teachers, even feeling uncomfortable, to gain insights into the communities in which we teach and our students' ways with words.

However, teachers willing to become informed about these issues must place their learning aside during scripted lessons.

YOUR THOUGHTS

Well, I said it was a short chapter. It's sad that there aren't examples of ways in which the phonics program cultivates children's and teachers' understandings of language variations and the relationships between language and culture. Culture is a political issue. I hope you are feeling that the definition of reading within a program, the view of the child, the view of the teacher, and the view of curriculum are political issues, too. But how political are they? Why are they political? Who gains? How?

8

Phonics, Reading, and Politics

Teacher burnout is not necessarily a symptom of excessive effort, of being overworked. It is the condition of not knowing why we are doing what we are doing. Burnout is the evidence of helplessness, of no longer being able to find a positive answer to the sigh, "What's the use?"

—Van Manen (1986, p. 29)

TEACHING IS POLITICAL

Teacher burnout is not about being tired. It is about feeling powerless. As you read this chapter, you may feel powerless or even helpless. Or angry. Or sad. But it is important to learn about the political side of teaching a direct systematic, intense scripted program and to understand our position as educators. We have to be articulate about our ways of teaching so we don't feel helpless. By learning about the political nature of teaching, we can shed the feeling that we are succumbing to some invisible force that takes the life, passion, joy, and spirit out of our teaching and our students' learning. The "use" (in answer to, "What's the use?") is our minds, our children's minds, and our futures. That's a positive answer to the sigh, "What's the use?"

This chapter may feel like a roller coaster ride. You may read it and think that I am a conspiracy theorist who believes that there are evil forces working in some underground fashion to hurt teachers and children. Politics does feel like a roller coaster ride, and teachers' and children's lives are saturated with the results of many political agendas. Different groups have different agendas, and we, as educators, feel the heat of those agendas. But this is no

97

conspiracy theory. Rather there are well-articulated political agendas. That means that supposed facts and figures are used in certain ways to cultivate and perpetuate certain agendas—agendas like vouchers, school choice, and (for some) the dismantling of public education. My mother says that, "Figures can't lie but liars can figure." I don't think that those with agendas are lying. I think that interests and desires are expressed in **political activity** that places blame on one thing, group, or point of view to achieve an agenda. Cambourne (2000) explained how political activity on educational agendas is carried out:

> Organisations which want to generate grassroots movements to support their agendas need to do at least these three things: 1) create a communal mindset of crisis about some highly-valued aspect of the culture [reading achievement on tests]; 2) identify a scapegoat which can be blamed for the crisis [whole language or the lack of teaching phonics]; 3) have a readily available remedy [for] the crisis [that also will] neutralise the scapegoat [programs like the one Karen must use]. (p. 10)

Someone (or ones) must gain from the adoption of phonics programs or those programs would disappear. It is in understanding the dynamics of power that are involved in such adoptions that we begin to understand the positions of teachers and children in those dynamics. In this chapter, I work at understanding the politics of reading instruction with particular emphasis on why and how political activity gets expressed as the adoption of phonics programs. In chapter 9, I discuss actions we have taken and can take to have our voices heard in political arenas.

POLITICS, POWER, AND POSITIONING

Most teachers don't like to consider their work as being political, but it is. Almost all work is political in some way, although we usually prefer to deny that teaching is political. After all, isn't teaching based on and in our love for children? How could that be political?

The answer is simple to write but complicated when I move to analyses of that simple answer. Simply put, teaching reading is political because it has to do with power. It has to do with power because decisions are made that influence what will happen in classrooms during the teaching of reading. For decisions to influence classrooms, power has to be exerted in some way. When the district office made a decision to purchase and mandate a phonics curriculum for every kindergarten through third-grade classroom, power was being exerted. It was being exerted on children and teachers. Power was exerted on the district by the newspapers, by other states spreading their panic at supposedly lower test scores, by the state board of education, by legislators, and even by some religious groups (Spring, 1997). Yet power can only be exerted when certain individuals are in a position to exert the power and others are in a position that demands that they relinquish to the power. Karen felt vulnerable, as most teachers do, to her principal, district administrators, the state board of education, and the state legislature.

Differences in power are *real* because we believe them to be real; they *feel* real, and we can list reasons that they are real. I am not making light of power, especially when it is perceived as power over us. Karen can list the reasons that she must comply to the district's demands. She says, "I love children . . . they are what I do. . . . I love teaching and learning. . . . I need this job [for income and insurance]." Karen understands her position in the power dynamics of the district.

Positioning is our understanding of where we fit in power hierarchies. I find the idea of positioning useful in explaining and understanding these power dynamics. At the same time, our positions are imposed on us and constructed by us; our positions have to do with our knowledge and understanding of our place, our potential for impact on that place, and our potential to sustain that impact. There are two groups of people whose positions I consider closely in this chapter. One group is teachers, Karen being a representative of that group. The other group is the students in Karen's classroom and classrooms in other districts that are adopting similar programs. The two groups are, of course, related in many ways, including their positions in the power dynamic of the school district.

TEACHERS' AND STUDENTS'
COMPLIANT POSITIONS

Karen's position is one of compliance, but she is not alone in this compliance. Teachers of young children have a history of compliance (Brady, 1995) sprinkled with some progressive educators who work to position themselves as informed and thoughtful educators. They are willing to face adversity to have teaching and learning as more democratic (Shannon, 1990) or even liberatory processes (Shor & Freire, 1987), in which inequities get named and addressed.

Children's positions are at the lowest endpoint of the hierarchy. They are viewed, particularly in phonics programs like the one Karen is forced to use, as recipients. This is a constructed position of powerlessness in which publishers view children as objects expected to absorb the delivered curriculum. This is a political position in which children are enslaved by curriculum and teachers are coerced into or agree to complicity.

HOLD IT! Stop right there! What did I just write? Children are enslaved by curriculum . . . teachers are complicit in that; now isn't that pushing it just a bit? Isn't that just a bit melodramatic?

No.

Look at the evidence. Consider the behaviors of Karen's children during the lesson. In other research in which a researcher spent an entire year observing phonics lessons (Udell, in prep.), the children's behaviors became increasingly asocial. The teacher had an increasingly difficult time keeping the students focused unless he became quite assertive (which was not easy and did not happen frequently). In other words, as teachers become cognizant that their students are enslaved to a curriculum that is holding them (teachers and students) hostage, the teachers relinquish some control (their power) of the classroom because they cannot face themselves as enslavers. The sadder option is when teachers comply to a mandate and then force children to comply with inappropriate curriculum. This deprofessionalizes the teachers.

The important thing for teachers to consider is their position in the curriculum hierarchy. If a teacher is satisfied with her or his position, that's his or her choice. But satisfaction or dissatisfaction must be rooted in consciousness of their positions and the positions of their students.

The positioning of teachers in the power hierarchy of the district, state, and national scenes can be understood from a variety of perspectives. When we seek to understand power hierarchies and positioning, some underlying and driving questions are:

- **Who is gaining?**
- **What are they gaining?**
- **How do they go about gaining?**
- **At whose expense are they gaining? (Who loses if someone wins?)**
- **How does their gain perpetuate a distribution of wealth and power that leaves some individuals out of access to an enhanced quality of life?**

These questions nag at the power hierarchies that exist. They are a frame for looking at situations deeply and politically to understand the distribution of power and the assigning and assuming of positions. The questions are useful in holding up a mirror to ourselves, our own positions, our perceptions of our power, and our moral and ethical responsibilities to children in classrooms as our understanding of all this is enhanced. A real balance of power in the teaching of reading is a balance of authority and position that supports teachers as responsible decision makers. But this balance is "*not* what is being mandated by politicians and administrators in various states and locales across the country" (Weaver, 1998, p. 12). The balance proposed by many politicians and administrators is going to "push us further in the direction of skills and away from meaningful and critical reading" (Weaver, 1998, p. 12). Their balance is going to leave teachers less powerful and in the position of not being able to use their professional knowledge in the day-to-day operation of their classrooms. As you read the following sections, consider the questions, sources of (perceived or *real*) power, your position, and the positions of children.

THE DEFINITION OF READING
IS A POLITICAL STATEMENT

Willis (1997) suggested that we examine how "changes in the definitions and purposes of literacy . . . have evolved in response to changes in the history of the United States" (p. 387). This means that the definition of reading changes over time and intimates that a definition is a political statement. It is political because it changes reflective of the people, contexts, and relationships involved. The definition of reading changes and is political because of issues of power and access that are involved and because of our increasing understanding of those issues. For example, when I was younger, I was forced to attend Hebrew school twice a week. We learned to *say* Hebrew. By "say" I mean that we were told the sounds of the letters and told how to blend those into Hebrew words, but we were taught Hebrew as a sound system. We never learned the meanings of anything that we were saying. Although I can open any prayer book and say the Hebrew that is in it, I am not reading it. I'm not reading it because I do not know what the sounds mean. Some prayer books provide translation, but I can never argue about the translation. I can only make the sounds to say the Hebrew. I can never (unless I start to study Hebrew for meaning) undertake a conversation in Israel with someone who wants to speak to me in

Hebrew. I am not a reader of Hebrew, but only a sayer of the words. I am not a member of the literate Hebrew-speaking community although I can say the sounds. Just because I say the sounds, I am not reading.

My parents were proud whenever I "read" Hebrew in our synagogue, but I was not reading. My schooling in the Hebrew language excluded me from participating in the Hebrew-speaking community because of the nature of that schooling. I participated in various Jewish rituals, but did not have full access to those speaking Hebrew. My definition of reading Hebrew differs from the definition of my Hebrew school teacher. She taught that being a "sayer" of sounds is being a reader of Hebrew. My definition of being a reader of Hebrew demands that I be a meaning-maker within a culture in which a language is used. This is a political shift in thinking of the definition of reading because it involves a shift in access to or relationships with others (Hebrew speakers), access to texts (written in Hebrew), and access to contexts (situations in which using Hebrew relates to my position with others).

When the children in Karen's class experience language during phonics, they are learning the way I learned Hebrew. Edelsky (1996) wrote that, "The difference between literacy as reading and literacy as NOT-reading refers to whether or not the reader *aims* to make a text meaningful for himself or herself" (p. 86; italics added). When a child is deprived of that "aim," the act of deprivation is a political act. When we present children with a definition of reading, as operationalized by the reading programs we use in school, we influence that aiming. When a definition of reading is that reading is the calling of nonwords, children cannot aim for meaning. The sad part is that Karen knows she is complicit in denying her students' aim when she uses precious class time to teach that reading is not a process of making sense or meaning.

We must help children understand the relationships between letters and sounds. However, when we reduce reading to *only* those relationships, we have lost what Bill Martin Jr. (1991) called, "the satisfaction of the sweeping, strong, beautiful syntax of a story or poem, a flush of language that continues uninterrupted by carrying its own thought, creating its own anxiety, offering its own perspective" (p. 133). A definition suggests what students and teachers will do and what can be expected from them. A definition implies what individuals will have access to and what they will be denied. If reading is the calling of words and sounds, we don't necessarily need fine literature to teach reading. We certainly don't need thoughtful responses, beauty, "a flush of language," or joy. Reading becomes work. Do the work, get the job done, move on to the next piece of work. Reading becomes a factory where the product is not a child as a reader. The product is the score that the child, the class, the school, the district, and the state attain on a test. The definition of reading is reduced to the potential for a score, not the potential to read for knowing, for joy, for learning, for locating information, or for becoming a contributing and thoughtful member of the democratic process. Yes, a definition is political, and all of our teaching actions are expressions of our definition.

Some researchers, politicians, and others with a conservative agenda suggest that if children know the sounds and can say words, they will be readers. But this is a simplistic definition that denies the bigness of reading. Willis and Harris (2000) explained that those living in poverty, both children and their families,

> know that learning to read will not ensure a more equitable or socially just world. They are not swayed by the spin doctors' myths that literacy learning will bring equality; they understand that greater systemic changes are needed in society and education. (p. 83)

This means that a definition of reading must include conscientization (Freire, 1970a) or the raising of consciousness around the idea of being a reader who reads the world in which she or he lives (as well as the word).

Historically, depriving the slaves in America of reading is rooted in an understanding of a definition of reading. It is not only about joy; it is about seeing, as Freire suggested. Reading is about understanding one's power and position and the political machinery that puts and maintains individuals in certain places in our society.

Yes, children need to know the sounds of the letter <a>, but they also need to have that <a> positioned in texts that are relevant to them—in their lives, their communities, and their cultures (Flores-Dueñas, 1997). For many dominant culture children, the intense focus on phonics is diluted by the richness of their at-home literacy environments. Their definitions of reading are elaborated by the mainstream uses and functions of literacy they experience at home (Darling-Hammond, 2000) in ways that support their achievement in mainstream ways (on tests). Recall that Karen's district's scores followed socioeconomics, with the richer areas scoring better on tests. Operationally, the curriculum is sorting children who are bound for success and those that are not, and it is doing so as a function of socioeconomic status (SES) and family level of education. It becomes our work as educators to sensitize ourselves to ways in which definitions limit success and also to ways in which we can teach reading to meet the needs of the diverse students we see in schools (see Au, 1993).

CURRICULUM IS A POLITICAL STATEMENT

Curriculum is more than a set of materials. Curriculum, in Karen's case, signifies many decisions that were made. Karen was not included in those decisions, but she and her students must live with them—a view made clear to her by her administrators in the school and district.

Curriculum is political because it comes from some *place* and that place is a place (position) of influence and power. The claims that children can't read, aren't learning to read, schools must be bigger (read: more economical), and that all children must experience the same curricular materials (Wilson, 2000) are all serving someone. They are serving curriculum manufacturers, politicians who are serving individuals who want to do away with public schools (Ohanian, 2000), religious groups (Spring, 1997), and legislators who answer to industry (which supports their election). This is what Wilson (2000) called the "Emperor's new education" (p. 334). However, "unlike the small child who exposed the Emperor's nudity, in a related folk tale, no one has succeeded in exposing the Emperor's new education" (p. 334).

But I'm trying to expose it—its undemocratic views, its deprofessionalizing stances toward teachers, and its inhumane treatment of children. Paul (2000) reminded teachers to think about books like *The Giver* (Lowry, 1993), in which culture, differences, and even color are bleached away. Paul explained that "These are worlds uninhabitable to real people *who retain cultural memory* and who *recognize social conflict and complexity*" (p. 340; italics added). The phonics curriculum that Karen is using is creating uninhabitable literacy worlds for children. Any time we influence the worlds of children, we are making a political statement and engaging in political activity. The curriculum that is enacted is a political document because it touches children's and teachers' worlds. Karen "retain(s) cultural memory" and "recognizes social conflict and complexity" and this causes her pain—pain that I refer to as *curricular heartache*. It is a heartache born of the consciousness of a teacher knowing she can do better than the curriculum that is binding and limiting her and her students.

When a curriculum is enacted, it answers this question: What is a curriculum supposed to do? Perrone (1998) reminded us that "the content of schools seldom relates to what people in a particular community are worried about or care deeply about" (p. 61). He explained that much of what happens in schools is disconnected from the community and that the "disconnectedness trivializes much of what students are asked to learn" (p. 61). In previous school years, Karen saw her children become increasingly phonemically aware with the use of language activities that were relevant to the children. Now she and her students live with imposed irrelevance that ignores bodies of reading research.

When an approach to teaching reading discounts or dismisses huge bodies of research, such as the research on miscue analysis (Brown, Marek, & Goodman, 1996), *that* is a political act. Texas and California, two high-population states, influence the rest of the country when decisions are made in those states about the teaching of reading. They influence the rest of the country because publishers cater to high-population states, adjusting what is available for sale to meet the desires of those states' curriculum decision makers. The more publishers match the demands of the high-population states, the more money they make. Texas and California are known for statewide adoptions, meaning millions of dollars are at stake. When those two states became interested in more phonics instruction, publishers were quick to present programs to them (see Taylor, 1998). Those states made adoptions. Their adoptions were analyzed by Dressman (1999), who found that they "disregard or avoid . . . any research findings of the intervening 30 years that refute or adjust traditional beliefs about the efficacy of traditional practices" (p. 279). Dressman went on to say that:

> . . . these programs pay little if any attention to the communicative function of language, to the complex interrelations of the subcomponents of literacy, or to the agency of children as learners or of adults as teachers. Instead, they prescribe programs of explicit, systematic instruction in the traditional subcomponents of reading and writing plus prerequisite screening and intervention via phonemic/phonological awareness activities. . . . They tacitly maintain that literacy is a cognitive issue that demands an almost exclusively cognitive approach to its instruction. (p. 279)

Dressman went on to describe the tediousness of these programs, referring to "reading a story aloud occasionally to break the monotonous labor of learning to read as an *unnatural* act" (p. 280; italics added).

Who gains when learning to read is a monotonous unnatural act? The children who rarely experience reading in other contexts aside from school lose; those that hear excited family members read to them outside of school also lose, just not as severely. When a curriculum teaches that reading is unnatural, it is making a political statement because those who have little power, who send their children to school with dreams of accessing power in the form of a better quality of life, are forced to stay marginalized. Their children are being edged out, pushed out, turned off, and disenfranchised from reading. They learn that reading is dull, unnatural, irrelevant, and dismissive of their lives outside of school. This is political work. It is political work that sounds like it would take place in a part of the world in which human rights are ignored, violated, or abused. It is happening here.

MOST TEACHERS OF YOUNG
CHILDREN ARE WOMEN

Agency, in the context of this discussion, means the ways in which teachers believe that they can act and, indeed, do act based on their understanding of their position in the power structure. In the present curricular-political environment, Karen's agency has shifted. The mandate of the scripted phonics program represents a shift by the district in how they view Karen and in the trust they place in her. Formerly, they trusted her to make informed professional decisions about the teaching and learning of reading. In that context, her agency as a teacher was rooted in her understanding of the reading process and informed by her commitment to ongoing professional development. The adoption of the phonics program positions the teacher as an agent of the publisher and as a technician. This is an imposed shift in the view of teachers in the district and it has influenced Karen's agency.

Recall that Karen was told that she has a "personal problem" because it took her an hour or more to complete the daily phonics lessons. Historically, elementary school teachers have been women, and they have been controlled by "others" (Shannon, 1990). Perhaps this hasn't changed much if a district-level reading person believed that he had permission to make such a remark. He believed himself to be positioned in such a way that he was allowed to say such a thing to a teacher. I know he would not say that to the superintendent of the district if the superintendent tried to teach a phonics lesson and came to the reading person with the same concern about the length of time the lesson took. The district-level reading person (a man) silenced Karen with his remark. He knew he would silence her because he relied on his historic aura of power in the district.

The systematic silencing of women is well documented (Belenkey, Clinchy, Goldberger, & Tarule, 1986); such silencing in schools exists for teachers and students (Fine, 1987). Karen believes she cannot say anything, although she feels strongly about her efficacy as a teacher of reading. Karen is forced into a position of submission to a curriculum that is contrary to her worldview of teaching and learning. I have written elsewhere about the violence done to (mostly women) teachers in efforts to silence them (Meyer et al., 1998). I have also written about the ways in which a group of women took advantage of a more trusting environment that existed in a district and worked with children, families, and each other to enhance student and teacher learning. This group of teachers worked at ending the cellular (Lortie, 1975) nature of teaching that leaves teachers feeling isolated and silenced.

Karen felt silenced and isolated. When the district came on strong, she went along with the phonics program and, during phonics instruction, bracketed the knowledge that she has, placing aside all that she has learned from years of practice, study, conferences, courses, and reading. At first she pulled back from her relationships with colleagues, families, community members, professors, and her students. She deferred to the knowledge of others although she has much knowledge. "They told us that if kids don't have this program . . . even if they are already reading . . . they don't understand the code and so they don't understand what they're reading."

In other words, the pressure, pain, and awareness combined in ways that numb a teacher. All of her richness and wealth is discounted in the economy that is run by those that believe that knowledge is discovered at the top of some imaginary source and delivered to the bottom (children) via hollow and no-need-to-think technicians.

As I write this, I picture once again in my mind the water-filled eyes of my friend Karen as she looks over her students' heads at me. I see the pain in those eyes as the same pain I would have if forced to teach what was not good for my students, if forced to turn my back on all that I know and understand, if forced to act as if I could homogenize the school experiences of my students. This is the pain of feeling complicit with something that runs counter to our knowledge. It is also suggestive of a deeper collective pain of teachers coming to consciousness about their positions. I don't mean to downplay the joys of consciousness-raising. Rather, my intention is to portray it as the intense beginning of coming to know that leads to action.

Don't get too discouraged. Remember that Karen began reaching out. She still attended conferences, read, and began to talk more to others about the problem. There's hope, just not very much in this chapter. The purpose here is to understand the contexts. We can build hope and action from that understanding.

THE PRESS HURTS US

Berliner and Biddle (1995) discussed many instances in which the popular press hurt teachers and children in school. For example, when *A Nation at Risk* (National Commission on Excellence in Education, 1983) was published, no one questioned the fact that not one single research study is cited in the entire document. That document was and is used to claim that students' performances declined consistently over the past years. Berliner and Biddle explained in great detail that there has not been an appreciable decline in test scores on the National Assessment of Educational Progress, yet the press finds insignificant declines and reports them as significant. Berliner and Biddle suggested that right wing groups want to paint a negative picture of public schools. By presenting the public schools as failing, they are gathering support for vouchers and other vehicles for draining money from public schools and pouring it into private schools.

Who gains? The wealthy. When they are provided with a dollar-amount voucher, they can add more money to it to send their child to a quality private school. The children left in the public schools are the less well off. Or, if the less well off use their voucher dollars for private education, they will receive a low-quality private education because they cannot afford to add funds to the voucher. The rich remain rich and the poor suffer more as support to public school evaporates. But the reports that are used to paint negative pictures of public schools are not accurate representations of what is happening in many schools:

> To summarize, recent criticisms of American schools have often been bolstered by impressive claims of evidence that appeared, on first glance, to support arguments about our "troubled" schools. On closer examination, however, many of those claims have turned out to be garbage. (Berliner & Biddle, 1995, p. 171)

Teachers' and students' lives are nested in that garbage. When right wing think tanks scoop up the garbage and lay it at the doorsteps of classrooms like Karen's, the pressure to perform is increased. When local papers publish scores that do not paint the entire picture of the district, more pressure is put on Karen. The focus on the test scores becomes more intense, and many teachers change their teaching to accommodate the tests. In a very well-orchestrated series of events, children performing below average on the standardized tests are put in the spotlight and their teachers are put in the hot seat. They are accused of not teaching phonics, yet as Karen and every good teacher knows:

> It would be irresponsible and inexcusable not to teach phonics. Yet the media are having a field day getting the word out that many of us ignore phonics in the teaching of reading. It just isn't so. (Routman, 1996, p. 91)

Some radical right wing groups do not even want voucher money. They want the public school system dismantled so that parents will have ultimate say over their children's education with no input from the government. They see vouchers as a way of government maintaining control (Ohanian, 2000).

Yet the most accurate predictors of how well a student will do on a test are family income and family level of education, along with teacher preparedness (Darling-Hammond, 2000). Why doesn't the press announce that a more even distribution of wealth and dedication to the preparation of quality teachers will improve learning more than pressure that has nothing behind it but the intent to weaken or dismantle public schools (Cambourne, 2000)?

IT'S NOT ABOUT WHOLE LANGUAGE; IT'S ABOUT WHOLE COUNTRY

Altwerger (1998) wrote poignantly to present evidence that what is at hand is not a reading war, which whole language advocates are waging against phonics advocates (or which phonics advocates are waging against whole language advocates). This is not a battle in which research-based evidence is being presented to make a case for a particular way to teach reading to beginning readers.

> . . . this is not a battle of reason, fact, or evidence. This is not even a battle over reading instruction, classroom pedagogy, or the literacy development of our children. The American political and religious right is simply using language and literacy as a convenient and convincing cover . . . for their true agenda: to discredit, control, and privatize American public schools. They seek to perpetuate their historical role of preserving privilege and class in this country. (Altwerger, 1998, p. 175)

Altwerger (1998) explained how little the United States spends on public education compared to other industrialized nations. She pointed out that the number of poor is growing as fewer individuals have access to public health care. She presented the numbers that demonstrate that "minorities comprise a disproportional high percentage of the poorest income groups" in the United States (p. 177). The poor get poorer, increasingly isolated, and feel less and less necessary.

Why would industry and politicians invest so much in perpetuating districts' use of phonics programs? This is the part of what is occurring presently in education that teachers do not like to hear. Perhaps I seem too much like a conspiracy theorist; I am not. It does seem that many conservative politicians and many businesses are working to silence teachers and deprofessionalize teaching.

Progressive and holistic philosophies of teaching and learning have been critiqued and attacked for years. Dewey (1938) experienced this long ago, and progressive educators have felt attacked since (Shannon, 1990). One issue at hand is compliance. Systematic, intensive boxed programs demand teacher and student compliance. Yet industry seems to be constantly calling for workers that can think. That is true; but they only want a small number of those workers to be thoughtful (Ohanian, 1999). Gee, Hull, and Lankshear (1996) described it this way:

> We are heading towards a world in which a small number of countries and a small number of people within them will benefit substantively from the new capitalism, while a large number of others will be progressively worse off and exploited. (p. 44)

In other words, the new capitalism that we are facing is one in which large numbers of people must not be thoughtful and must be compliant. Karen and her students are learning to be compliant.

Karen was not free to make important pedagogical decisions informed by her knowledge of her students. Under the guise of scientific studies, her district office was holding up weak and confounded research and bullying her into conforming. She was forced to use a certain program, at a certain time, with all of her students. She was not allowed to decide who needed intensive phonics and who did not.

In stronger words, literacy is being used to commit acts of violence against teachers, students, and, ultimately, humanity. Stuckey (1991) discussed such violence this way when she viewed reading as:

> ... a social restriction and an individual accomplishment. Individuals read and write, or don't, and individuals do with their literacy what they can. The

subjectivities of minds, and the ways in which people make their lives and thoughts, and the ways in which people are coerced, entrapped, colonized, or freed, must be addressed as processes. At the same time, the processes must not become the issue, since the conditions for any process, and especially for the literacy process, determine the possible outcomes. That is why, for example, teaching literacy depends on the circumstances rather than on the textbook. Our attention needs to be focused on the *__conditions__* in every instance.

A theory of literacy is a theory of society, of social relationships; and the validity of a theory of literacy derives from the actual lives of the people who make the society. (p. 64; emphasis added)

Each part of Stuckey's ideas can be held up to the phonics program at hand. The children are developing individual and social understandings of what reading is. Those with limited reading activity at home are getting a very skewed notion of what reading is, how it is learned, and what it is for. There is a "theory of society, of social relationships" in the phonics program. It is reflective of the theory of society that demands that we have a class system and an obscene distribution of wealth in which the less fortunate are denied access to basic necessities such as health, decent diet, and well-being of mind.

Another part of that theory has to do with the idea of compliance. Ohanian (1999) pointed out that the largest employer in our country is Manpower. Manpower hires temporary workers that do not get benefits. If our economy is teaching us that we need a temporary labor force that must *comply* to the changing daily demands of capitalism, but reap few of the benefits beyond hourly wage, then the phonics program is training children for the workforce.

THERE *IS* A REAL CRISIS

A very poignant presentation of political agendas for education in the United States is Spring's (1997) book, *Political Agendas for Education: From the Christian Coalition to the Green Party*. In the book, he explained the many interests in American education and how they are using power to position themselves in ways to control the future of education. He discussed the religious right and their desire to "gain control of schools and the media [as] based on a belief that ideas determine social conditions [and that] crime is a result of learning immoral ideas, not conditions of poverty" (p. 5). He helps us understand the difference between the religious right and groups like the Heritage Foundation (and other conservative think tanks). He traced the involvement of conservative groups with government, industry, and universities. He also made it clear that, "The religious right rejects the idea of governments imposing national academic standards and testing. They want to rely on the authority of God" (p. 42). For some religious groups, gaining control of the schools is the work of God in an effort to bring (their) morality to the people of the country. For industry, the agenda is about influencing America's position in the global market; in other words it's about money. Spring's discussion helped me understand that, although the agenda may be the same, there are many groups' interests being expressed in those agendas for education.

Spring also discussed charter schools and drew distinctions between the ways different groups are trying to organize those schools. For some, the move is toward smaller schools in which students' needs and interests can be addressed. For others, the goal is to bring the school and school funding to the church. Spring explained that some charter laws will keep teachers protected in that licenses for teaching will still be required and teachers will be able to be members of unions. Other charter laws will not require licensure and will not provide teachers with tenure. He fears that teachers will lose union protection under some charter school laws as they are written. It becomes clear that some groups do want to dismantle public education to serve their own interests. Again, who gains when this occurs? The "haves" gain and the "have-nots" lose.

Public education is an essential part of being in a democratic country. Dismantling it leaves the poor poorer and leaves teachers unprotected and vulnerable to even lower salaries than they currently earn. Dismantling it has the potential for leaving children in classrooms with underqualified teachers and forces children to be compliant, at best, giving them the impression that they are disposable commodities.

Evidence of the investment of some in the dismantling of public education can be found in interesting places. For example, it is easier for inmates in California's correctional facilities to get to books than it is for children in public schools. The prison system is better served than the public schools when it comes to access to books because there are more books per capita in prisons than in public schools (McQuillan, 1998)! Putting greater access to reading in prison suggests less commitment to it in public schools.

The factors that have always influenced reading achievement continue to influence reading achievement: access to books, support in learning to read, family level of income, family level of education, and teacher competency (in understanding the reading process). When inmates have more access to books than students do in schools, we need to worry about priorities (McQuillan, 1998). When competent teachers' practices are tightly controlled and limited, we need to worry. When there's pressure on communities to initiate school-related policies and practices that will make the distribution of wealth (including educational wealth and wealth in terms of access) more uneven than it already is, we are in a crisis.

The "manufactured crisis" (Berliner & Biddle, 1995) in reading has led to a real crisis. The manufactured one suggests a simple solution for all the problems that confront our society: Teach phonics and it will all go away. Teach phonics directly, systematically, to all the children in your class at the same time in the same way and it will all go away. Teach children that putting the sounds together is reading and it will all go away. The real crisis is the learning-to-read lives of young children. For them, it is a crisis of identity, curriculum, voice, reading, teaching, and learning. It is a crisis in the teaching-of-reading lives of teachers. For teachers, it is a crisis of pedagogy, identity, curriculum, voice, reading, and learning.

My fear is that too many teachers will succumb to the pressure in this atmosphere of increased hysteria and control. Karen did so for the first year of the phonics program. Other teachers did so, too. Some of these teachers are beginning to respond to the mandate by planning to quietly rush through the scripted lessons, skipping parts and abbreviating sections. But others are first-year teachers who are being taught that this is the way to teach reading. They are gaining inservice credit in their district as they learn the limited and limiting techniques of these programs. Some are even getting graduate credit. They are buying into a type of classroom language learning environment that is a pressure cooker. Ohanian eloquently pointed out that there is no "one size fits all" curriculum in reading. If anything, what is happening now is a "one size fits few" curriculum (Ohanian, 1999). This is a curriculum that "gives nonstandard students no place to go" (p. 2). It is a curriculum in which teachers are under huge amounts of pressure to *cover* it all, where they "are eliminating recess and putting away the building blocks, the tempera paints, and the picture books that don't introduce phonemes in the sequence chosen by the publishing conglomerate" (Ohanian, 1999, p. 19).

The pressure to conform to higher standards is "as cynical as handing out menus to homeless people in the name of eradicating hunger"

(Ohanian, 1999, p. 31). When we keep raising the standards, more children fall under that standard. Now we'll watch as states punish those poorly performing schools by denying them funding, rather than providing additional support. If there is additional support, it will be to bring children up to the standards, the homogenized all-of-you-be-the-same standards that deny identity, culture, and voice in the curriculum. Yet as Ohanian pointed out, the push for higher standards because of the needs in the job market is a myth because "there aren't enough high-paying jobs to go around" (p. 108). The real crisis at hand is not about phonics. The real crisis is about teaching, learning, access, security, well-being, wealth, and quality of life.

STUDENTS AS POLITICAL ACTIVISTS

Most of the prior discussion focuses on the teachers' positions in an oppressive situation. What about the children? Dressman (1999) offered that,

> . . . in the 1990s what appears to be indisputably objective *scientific* knowledge about early literacy to some appears to others to be a set of discrete facts that have been broadly interpreted to produce policies and literacy curriculums that are as much the product of their makers' cultural politics and normative assumptions about social reality as they are the product of a dispassionate use of the scientific method. (p. 258)

Under the guise of science, students are objectified into a common pool in which they all must learn to swim at the same pace, with identical instruction and (in the program that Karen uses) with little systematic ongoing evaluation of their progress. They merely move from lesson to lesson in a daily program.

The children in Karen's class are ensconced in politics, just as their teacher is. The children are the objects of the curriculum, but they are also involved in political activity because they are acting on the curriculum setting in Karen's classroom. Some of the children are not comfortable with their position in the curriculum and they are acting on it. There are a few ways in which their actions may be interpreted.

One way to interpret their actions is that they have not assented (Kohl, 1991) to learn. Kohl presented a striking account of himself and others in situations in which, for a variety of reasons, they did not agree to (assent to) the teaching that was offered. In Karen's classroom, a setting in which instruction typically is appropriate for the language, culture, needs, and interests of the students, phonics is an aberration. It is a time of the day when all the norms that Karen and the children use for teaching and learning during other parts of the day are violated. I am suggesting that some of the students' behaviors are ways of resisting the mandate. The mandate does not fit the students' needs, interests, language, or culture. It does not fit their emerging reading identities. It does not fit their commitment to language as making sense and stories as being interesting and sparking a flame deep within. The children are engaging in political activity when their behavior is considered to be resistance. In this interpretation, they are acting as individuals in their nonparticipation in the curriculum.

Another interpretation is that not paying attention goes beyond saying *no* individually to the learning at hand. For some of the children, their acts of not engaging are a form of nonviolent civil disobedience. They are not just acting for themselves, they are acting as representatives for all (and with some) of their oppressed colleagues whom they want to liberate. I won't suggest that the students engaging in nonviolent civil disobedience could label their actions as such; that would be going a bit too far. But young children do have an intuitive sense of altruism, and they do know when someone (including themselves, but also others) is being oppressed or experiencing unfairness. The children who reach out to their colleagues, by talking to them, poking them, stroking their hair, or watching them engage in other behaviors, are making connections. Their connections are ways of drawing attention away from the phonics lesson and toward something meaningful—social interaction and meaningful relationships. If the textual activity cannot be meaningful, these students are the ones who seek social meaning by *some* type of interaction. This is political activity and they are political activists.

I know some readers have got to be wondering about this idea of first graders as activists engaged in nonviolent civil disobedience. The children love Karen and would never intentionally hurt her feelings. But the need for meaningful interaction around texts is strong for some children. They rely on Karen for it. When it is not there, they go into action. Carini (1979) said that children will set standards that surprise us, and that we need to be open to multiple interpretations of what children do to see such surprises. If we lock ourselves into conventional interpretations of classroom behavior, many of the children in Karen's classroom are "bad" or "poorly behaved during phonics," but if we open our thinking to other ways of understanding their behavior, even if it seems metaphorical, we see things differently. That's what I'm trying to do now. I'm trying to see things differently to honor children as thoughtful learners who genuinely expect things to make sense. If things don't make sense, the activist draws others to something that will make sense.

Of course, with enough experiences in some school settings, many will give that up. But the ones who are not giving up on sense and thoughtfulness as the stuff of schools are the ones who will perform acts of civil disobedience in settings like the phonics lesson. They're the children we need to watch as barometers of our teaching and the children's learning. They're also the ones who are discounted by the one-size-fits-all curriculum. They're the ones who are at risk because they will figuratively (and eventually literally) find no place for themselves in school. Where will they go? What will they do? What will they learn? Luis Rodriguez (1993) answered these questions in his autobiographical work, *Always Running. La Vida Loca: Gang Days in L.A.*:

> "The Crazy Life" in my youth, although devastating, was only the beginning stages of what I believe is now a consistent and growing genocidal level of destruction predicated on the premise there are marginalized youth with no jobs or future, and therefore, expendable. (pp. 6–7)

They will learn that they are expendable, replaceable at a low cost, and just not worth much.

GOT A HEADACHE?

The information in this chapter is a lot to fit into our heads. So many people seem to have interests in education, and those interests are expressed and realized in many different ways. Yet as I said earlier in this book, my faith lies in thoughtful teachers who can decide what children need. It is within those teachers' classrooms that my headache is relieved.

My faith lies in teachers coming to know the communities in which they live and perhaps coming to know along with their students as Kolbe (1999) did. As a sixth-grade teacher, he had his students study their community and write about what they learned. By transcribing audiotapes, developing written ethnographic records of their excursions into their community, and interviewing many members of their community, Kolbe's sixth graders began to read their worlds, and their reading test scores rose.

Kolbe was involved in political work and he knew it. Helping his students read their worlds became even more powerful as they began studying civil rights (T. Kolbe, personal communication). The students uncovered stories of how their parents arrived in the United States from war-torn countries; others uncovered what their families did during the 1960s civil rights movement in the neighborhoods around their school. The students connected to their community and became better readers and writers of texts because of the relevance of their work to their literacy learning.

This work is political, as we found out (Meyer et al., 1998) when we began our study group of primary teachers. Our work with young children as they inquired quite passionately into their interests disrupted the school in which we worked. Some teachers were angry at the intensity of the young children's learning; others discounted the children's work as not following the district objectives. Tensions grew, some relationships blossomed while others faltered, and our group kept meeting. We witnessed children's urgency in learning to read and write because they wanted to address their interests via reading and writing. Children's literacy became an integral part of finding and addressing myths that led them to being fearful where, they came to find, they didn't need to be afraid. Their emerging literacy became a tool they honed to learn about their worlds. They read because they were curious and they wrote because they had important things to share. Along the way, their teachers taught them what they needed to do that work. Their teachers taught them where to find information, how to sound out words, ways of recording data, the sound that <d> makes, and more. In the larger picture of reading and writing, the most minute details were addressed.

The details were addressed because the teachers were supported in making decisions about what to teach and when. They were allowed to use the basal if they wanted; they were allowed to shelve the basal if they wanted. They were treated as professionals who could make decisions. The principal made a strong political statement when he told the teachers that he trusted them to be experts. He was admitting that teaching and learning are complex, have specificity to the local contexts, and are relational in that they must reflect the relationships among teachers, students, and others in and around the school.

I have learned with teachers and children in schools that when the learning mattered, not for a test but for life, the learning got complex and authentic. When it got complex, many students' needs were addressed by a curriculum that had high, sensitive, and responsive standards. We don't seem to know how to or aren't able to get the stories of these teachers and children into the press. They linger in professional journals, but don't seem to influence the political dynamic that leads to an overreliance on standardized tests and the adoption of phonics programs that aren't meeting many children's needs.

YOUR THOUGHTS

My main goal in this chapter was to convince readers that teaching phonics is political activity. All of our decisions as educators, including the decision to not make decisions, are political. The decision to not make decisions means that you let someone else make all the decisions for you. It means that you've decided that you don't, won't, can't, or deny that you know your students well enough to make decisions about their educational experience. If that's not a comfortable place for you, it's time to think about acting.

How are the decisions made by and for schools in which you have interests? Who gains by those decisions? How? Who loses? How? Who has voice in the decisions and who is excluded? Where are you as an activist for children, teachers, and curriculum?

9

Teachers, Activism, and Hope

This time, the sky really is falling.

—Ohanian (2000, p. 355)

WE, TOGETHER

Maybe it is. It certainly feels that way to Karen as curriculum restraints become tighter and tighter and she begins to envision herself as someone who has to go underground with her teaching. When she sees her newest colleagues forced to use the basal for the first 3 years of their teaching, as well as being forced to use the phonics program, she tends to quietly retreat to her classroom. If she does this, she becomes a teacher-hermit who can only celebrate what she is doing with those she trusts deeply. She becomes a singularity, isolated, alone.

In this chapter, I use the word "we" quite a bit. That's because I am a teacher, too. And I am a researcher. Although I haven't focused on my own teaching and research agenda specifically, both are being influenced by the phonics curricula being imposed around the country. As I said at the beginning of the book, I never thought I'd be writing a book about phonics. Yet here I am, doing just that. My research on the influence of these types of programs came about as a response to my love of teachers like Karen and to increased pressure to do research that does not tell the stories of real teachers in real classrooms (see Taylor, 1998). Taylor discussed the push toward "reliable replicable research" that does not allow for individual differences. I see this as part of the push toward uniformity, compliance, and homogeneity. In other words, don't be different.

My response is, **we**. WE will be different. We will strive toward uniqueness. We will honor the differences among students, teachers,

119

schools, and communities. We will work toward democratic ideals and not toward compliance. We will have high and honorable goals for all learners, but this will not be a standardized set of outcomes or performances. My use of "we" in this chapter represents a move toward an end to the isolation that works against us and a move toward solidarity with those of us who are willing to get smarter and deal with some of the pressures we are under as thoughtful teachers and learners.

GETTING SMARTER

Teachers are smart. We know about children, ourselves as teachers, learning, curriculum, culture and its relevance to teaching and learning, the communities in which we teach, and curriculum. We understand ways in which all of these areas overlap and influence a child's identity as a reader (and our own identity as teachers). Karen is interested in getting smarter, and teachers like Karen are also interested in getting smarter. Informed teachers can address some of the political rhetoric that is aggressively held in front of us. Getting smarter about things like the reasons for the manufactured crisis in education and getting smarter about the ways in which power is distributed within a district can lead to informed and safe action. I don't want Karen or teachers like her to get fired. If they are fired or forced to quit, the teachers who remain become quieter, silenced. Lather (1991) discussed the importance of understanding authority when she wrote that, "To deconstruct authority is not to do away with it but to learn to trace its effects, to see how authority is constituted and constituting" (p. 144).

Lather (1991) suggested that authority (and I would say *power* as well) is put together in a certain way and functions in certain ways. I would add that part of that functioning is contributing to the constitution of our teaching and children's learning identities. Teachers need to understand how authority is constituted so that we can understand ways in which we are being influenced by that authority. In other words, we have to understand the power structure and our positions within that structure. With that information, we can begin to think about how to act safely within and on the structures influencing our practice.

DON'T ACT ALONE

John Dewey (1904) wrote:

> If teachers were possessed by the spirit of an abiding student of education,
> this spirit would find some way of breaking through the mesh and coil of cir-
> cumstance and would find expression for itself. (1904, NSSSE Yearbook)

The *expression* of *spirit* leads to the idea of teachers as activists whose
spirits move them to understand their positions and to work at changing
those positions if they are not fair, not just, not equitable, and not respectful of teaching as a profession. Yet if it is difficult for teachers to face the
political nature of the profession, how will we be moved to action?

Before responding to that question with particular strategies, one note
of caution: *Do not act alone.* Anyone who acts alone in the present climate
is easily eliminated, usually by tactics that are within the bounds of their
district's jurisdiction. In other words, no laws will be broken, but you will
be removed. For example, a teacher that acts alone may be asked to move
from teaching kindergarten to teaching sixth grade. If a principal knows
that the teacher is a primary grade expert, the move may be within the
rights of the district, but it may be distasteful enough to the teacher that she
or he leaves or acquiesces to some pressure being exerted.

Kathleen Mason (1999) knows what this feels like. When she returned
to teaching after a yearlong sabbatical leave, she was assigned to teach
first grade in a "back to basics" school. She tried to live out her progressive beliefs, but her teaching assignment was void of the supportive community she had at her previous school. She wrote, "I left the classroom. I
could not fight the system alone any longer. My health, energy, and passion were fading" (p. 21). Although her fight wore her down, she did learn
not to try it alone. When asked about getting involved in the politics of
teaching, she responded, "As I sit in the warehouse cleaning science kits,
counting the minutes, I wonder . . . How can we not [act]?" (p. 21). Mason
moved to a nonteaching position in the district, but she remains committed
to political activism.

We need to move cautiously, getting smarter by paying attention to the
distribution of power and finding colleagues who will begin to think and
eventually act with us. This may take some time as you get to know each
other in new ways—political ways.

TALKING WITH EACH OTHER

Begin by conversing informally with others that you know within and beyond your school. Perhaps you'll meet for coffee one morning before or
after school or on a weekend. Maybe you'll have a Friday Afternoon Club

(FAC) at a local restaurant. Maybe you'll share some ideas at such a meeting, but these need to be informal with no strong directions established too soon. Get to know each other's understandings of the power in the district, your views about reading and teaching and learning, and your understandings of the position of teachers and children in the district. Get to know your beliefs about what teachers should be able to do as decision makers.

Ellen Brinkley (with Weaver, Campbell, Houston, Williams, Little, Mohaghan, Freedman, Bird, & Bird, 1997) began with such conversations and soon developed a group called *Michigan for Public Education*. They needed a group that would gear up and act quickly because progressive teaching practices in the state were at stake. This group consisted of a university researcher (and parent), parents, librarians, teachers, and other citizens of the state. All members were concerned about the state's move toward curriculum that put aside much of the learner-centered practice that was an essential part of the reading curriculum in many of the schools in the state. Michigan, like other states, was experiencing systematic "attacks on public education" (p. 537). There was a conservative push toward "basics," which meant that teachers who were successful in teaching phonics, spelling, and grammar "in the context of reading and writing" (p. 537) would not be able to continue doing so. Michigan was also experiencing negative sentiment toward multicultural education, and there were increased efforts at censoring books from schools.

The group didn't agree with the way the schools were being portrayed in the popular press nor did they subscribe to the conservative agendas arising at the state board of education and in the state legislature. They admit that "none of us had much background as political activists, but we all had a passionate commitment to our cause" (p. 538). Their work involved connections with other groups so that they would not stand alone. They recount finding and working with various organizations: People for the American Way, Americans for Religious Liberty, Michigan Public Education Task Force, League of Women Voters, Michigan Education Association, American Association of University Women, and the American Civil Liberties Union (p. 539). They began a Web site and a newsletter, and they developed pamphlets for others to read. Their intense efforts exhausted them, of course, but paid off as the conservative agenda was shelved. I encourage you to read their story in *Language Arts* (1997, November; vol. 74, no. 7).

Bess Altwerger (1998) presented some of the work that she and some community members are doing in Maryland at the Whole Language Umbrella Conference. They are facing a conservative newspaper that publishes negative reports about teaching reading that Bess and her group are working to counter by writing pamphlets and distributing them. That group is also organizing for other ways to respond.

In the fall of 1998, the first National Conference for Public Education was held in Washington, DC. Many of the national professional organizations (International Reading Association, National Council of Teachers of English, National Council of Social Studies, etc.) were represented at this conference. The goal was to issue broad and resounding support for public education.

Another example of not acting alone that has reached some fruition occurred in Florida, when the state's voucher system was ruled to be unconstitutional according to the state's constitution. The ruling to remove vouchers as a way of funding a child's education was supported by "a coalition that includes Florida Education Association/United teachers union, the National Association for the Advancement of Colored People and a handful of families and educators" (Hallifax, 2000).

There are not many accounts of well-orchestrated responses to conscrvative agendas because those teachers who are involved are so busy teaching and developing responses that they don't have time to publish their accounts. As I meet at national conferences with colleagues from many states, I hear more stories of groups of teachers and supporters of public education meeting to organize so that the voices of opposition to programs like the one Karen must use can be heard. A crucial part of this activity is that it begins with people talking to each other.

TELL YOUR STORIES . . .
AGAINANDAGAINANDAGAIN

One year when I was teaching second grade, a new curriculum arrived at our school. The focus of the curriculum was helping children report whether they had been sexually abused. We talked a lot about touching and whether the touching felt okay or not okay. The children were told (in second-grade words) to trust their intuitions. If they felt that something that was happening to them made them think, *Uh oh, this is not right*, they were to tell someone and keep telling different people until someone listened. The curriculum was acknowledging that some adults did not believe (or dismissed as an overreaction) children when they reported certain incidents. Our message was this: Keep talking until someone listens.

The connection to our present plight in teaching is this: Keep talking until someone listens. Talk to colleagues, families who have loved your teaching, friends, legislators, and anyone else whose support might enhance your position as a professional. Remember to understand, as much as possible, your present position so that you don't make yourself too vulnerable. (And don't act alone.)

One of the most powerful activities in which teachers can engage is meeting with each other. The purposeful and systematic overcoming of the cellular and isolated nature of teaching (Lortie, 1975) is a powerful tool for activism. Teachers' lives include significant interaction with children; rarely are they encouraged to meet and discuss with other teachers. Inservice days are typically tightly planned to meet district agendas. It's time to meet and engage in discussions. We need to tell our stories to understand what is happening to us. This reminds me of the beginning of the film, *A River Runs Through It* (Redford & Markey, 1992), in which the narrator begins this way:

> Long ago, when I was a young man, my father said to me, "Norman, you like to write stories?"
> And I said, "Yes, I do."
> Then he said, "Some day, when you're ready, you might tell the story of our family. Only then will you understand what happened and why."
> (Columbia Tri-Star Pictures, 1992)

In our discussions with each other, we have the opportunity to see how each of us understands what is happening and why. We can hear each other's stories and look for the "why" so that we can begin to think about *how* we might act. In the telling of our stories, we can begin to understand our positions, the structures of power, and our thoughts about our students' (and our) learning lives.

Ohanian (1999) put it quite eloquently:

> . . . we teachers can resist the . . . imperative that would turn us into train conductors, programmed to keep our students operating on an ideal schedule devised by a complicity of politicians and bureaucrats. As teachers, we must resist much. We must also tell [our] stories. We must tell them often, and we must tell them loudly. (p. 24)

Ohanian is suggesting that we eventually move to telling our stories beyond the forums of teachers. I wonder how the families of Karen's students would respond to the phonics lesson presented in chapter 2. As they listened to the litany of nonlearning behaviors, I wonder how surprised, frustrated, and even enraged they might become. I wonder if they would begin to think that the push to teach systematic, direct, intense phonics to an entire class is not the silver bullet they were told it would be. If Karen presented chapter 2 to parents, what might they ask her? I wonder if they would ask her what she, a respected teacher with a history in the community, thought was best for the children. If they asked that question, Karen could answer by pointing to each family and telling stories of their children, demonstrating her understanding of their children's learning lives and her knowledge of how to teach reading.

In his book, *In Defense of Good Teaching*, K. Goodman (1998) opened a forum for stories to be told. This book contains 11 of the most riveting stories you'll read about teaching and learning. More than ever, after reading this book, you'll know that the push for phonics programs like the one Karen is using is about much more than the teaching of letter–sound correspondence. For example, in one chapter, Edelsky (1998) wrote that,

> The far right's love affair with phonics is a tactic, not a goal. They tout the benefits of phonics, but what they are really pushing is control of teachers, texts, and readers in a universe of moral absolutes. (p. 39)

In K. Goodman's book, David and Bonnie Freeman (1998) discussed the ways that California changed in its definition of reading in response to a complex set of problems (some discussed earlier, such as access to books). One important part of their chapter is their description of the political machinery that moved into gear to undermine a state document that gave teachers much control in their classrooms. They also explained why that document could not do what it was supposed to do. The long arm of "moral absolutes" was reaching out and shaking California's teachers and students, and the Freemans are telling the story.

Allington and Woodside-Jiron, both in K. Goodman's (1998) book and in another research journal (1999), told the story of a document known as "Thirty Years of Research" (Grossen, 1997), which supposedly explains *all* there is to know about the teaching of reading. Their work is one of debunking what Grossen reported; they explain that few of her findings were actually bolstered by the research she cited. Still Grossen's document was widely circulated and contributed to some states' decisions about program adoptions. Allington and Woodside-Jiron (1999) also discussed the research supported by the National Institute for Child Health and Development (NICHD) and concluded that, in our estimation, the available NICHD-supported research provides neither sufficient guidance to recommend whole-scale reform of the general education early literacy curriculum nor support for the instructional recommendations offered in the Grossen (1997) white paper. (p. 10)

All of the ways of telling stories, from FAC meetings to debunking of documents presented as The Truth, help us find others who will support our thinking and work toward some collective actions.

Summarizing thus far, you can act when you:

⇒ Read and discuss other's stories.

⇒ Tell your own stories.

⇒ Analyze each other's stories.

⇒ Get smarter.

⇒ Find some support in other colleagues, friends, organizations, and families.

⇒ Plan strategies for action. (Keep reading, I'm going to discuss these next.)

MOVING BEYOND STORIES:
SOME STRATEGIES

In this and the following sections, I introduce strategies you can use to support teachers' academic freedom as professional decision makers.

Voting

One of my fantasies, as we face the growing number of state legislatures that are forcing programs into classrooms, is that masses of teachers and other supporters of teaching as a profession gather outside of their state capital buildings and silently wave their voter registration cards. We need to show our presence by casting a vote. Perhaps you can be part of a group that writes a state bill offering teachers professional freedom to choose programs that meet the needs of their students. W.E.B Du Bois (1969) knew the power of the vote:

Save the great principle of democracy and equal opportunity and fight segregation by wealth, class or race or color, not by yielding to it but by watching, visiting and *voting* in all school matters, organizing parents and children and bringing every outside aid and influence to co-operate with teachers and authorities. (p. 126; emphasis added)

"Co-operation" means we do not necessarily agree with authorities (*cooperate*, with no hyphen), but we do operate at the same time (co-operate) to enlighten different points of view. Our actions must always include the democratic idea and ideal of acceptance of the expressions of diverse points of view. Yes, I know that gets abused at times. But what works any better?

Supporting Representation

We can organize by supporting candidates for the local school board; state school board; and local, state, and national legislatures. We need to make sure we have a voice in putting forth candidates or running ourselves. We need to participate in unions or other organizations, where we may gain voice for children. Yearly dues for a teacher's membership in teacher associations or unions is usually in the hundreds of dollars. If you're not being represented in ways that you like, act on that misrepresentation by letting your unions know that you are dissatisfied. Encourage your colleagues to do the same. Some teachers are resigning their union memberships as a show of dissatisfaction. Make sure that you understand all that your union provides before you resign. For example, some unions provide liability insurance. Some teachers may find more comprehensive (and not as expensive) liability insurance from other sources. Get the facts, voice your opinion, and encourage your colleagues to voice their opinions. Then see how the organization responds: Does it study the ways it represents you? Does it decide whether that representation sufficiently reflects your point of view? Does the organization's actions warrant your continued membership?

Comply, Resist, Infiltrate

P. David Pearson (2000) offered three responses to policies that districts or states (or others) enact. He said that we might **comply**, **resist**, or **infiltrate**. These are strategies that you can consider as you engage with a group of colleagues and others interested in becoming more active. Compliance is a strategy I've discussed, although I don't view it as a positive strategy in that it only serves to perpetuate the power and positions that already exist.

The many strategies that are discussed next are about resistance. The idea of infiltration is based on the idea of subversion. In other words, Pearson suggested that you enter the "policy culture" to change that culture. This might involve you becoming a principal, district administrator, legislator, or union representative from your school to effect change. Some teachers infiltrate on a very local level by not teaching what they have been directed to teach; this is infiltration rooted in subversion. You have to decide whether any of these three are directions you want to consider as an activist (although again, the first is not too risky and not too useful in terms of changing curriculum). Rather than focus on broad responses such as "resistance," what follows are some specifics for action.

STRATEGIES FROM AND FOR SUCCESSES

Some of the groups that have met with success and published their stories (and other activists) offer ideas for action. In this section, I present some of their suggestions. For a more in-depth explanation of these, you can check the sources I cite (most of which are available at your local college or university library or may even be in your school or district library or media center if they have a professional development section).

Michigan for Public Education

Brinkley et al. (1997) found the following strategies helpful in working to "strengthen public education":

⇒ Talk to others in existing groups. . . . Work as a task force . . . within an already established organization to focus on needs.

⇒ Start with a handful of people and coffee and rolls in someone's living room. [They report that groups began this way in Texas, Arizona, and Ohio.]

⇒ Think through the issues carefully. [Tell a lot of stories and analyze them.] Don't get frustrated too quickly. It took us several months of discussion, reading, investigation, and more discussion before we could articulate a very clear sense of direction and purpose.

⇒ Don't be afraid to speak out about controversial topics. Take someone with you so you're not alone.

⇒ Write out "talking points" ahead of time before speaking, priori-tizing the most important points you want to make. [Avoid jargon.]

⇒ Take multiple copies of any formal or written statement you plan to read in a public forum and distribute them to members of the board or groups you're speaking to and to the press if they're in attendance.

⇒ Encourage others to express their views by providing them with brief, easy-to-read information that highlights a particular problem or need. Provide addressees, e-mail, phone, and fax numbers [of key decision makers].

⇒ Take a stand on targeted issues that are most important in your area. By polarizing viewpoints, you may help audiences see contrasts and alternative possibilities; but by publicly characterizing other posi-tions as extremist, you may lose as many or more supporters than you gain.

⇒ Seek out coalition and network groups that share similar or related concerns about public education.

⇒ "Just do it." We all know why we just can't get involved. . . . Make The Time. . . . Get political! . . . Every voice is needed to defend pub-lic education and the democratic process that sustains it. (p. 541)

Brinkley's group in Michigan (called Michigan for Public Education [MPE]) also learned about the Freedom to Learn Network (FLN) in Penn-sylvania and connected with them to learn some of their strategies. Brinkley et al. reported that the FLN has yearly conferences that make a difference in Pennsylvania. MPE used many of FLN's strategies and their own, as well, to come up with the prior list. These kinds of connections among groups are important so that groups do not feel that they are iso-lated pockets of action. The connections are made possible by someone's willingness to tell the story of their group publicly, as Brinkley et al. did in their *Language Arts* article.

Teachers Save a Program

One good example of a group that worked together to respond to a local need is described in the book *You Can Make a Difference: A Teacher's Guide to Political Action* (Keresty, O'Leary, & Wortley, 1998). The au-thors described their successful efforts to save a literacy program that they demonstrated was successful for the children in their district. They are a fine example of not acting alone. They worked with other teachers and gathered survey data from families that supported the literacy program. The teachers in this book explain how they used their survey data, information from researchers, and their own knowledge of the children in their schools to present a case to the school board and anyone else who would listen. They include examples of press releases, the parent survey, and more in helpful appendixes.

Whose Business Is Teaching Reading?

In her book on organizing for change, *Teachers Organizing for Change, Making Literacy Learning Everybody's Business*, Cathy Fleischer (2000) presented what she learned by studying ways in which community organizers and social activists work to bring about change. She presented organizing lessons from people like Candy Lightner, who organized Mothers Against Drunk Driving (MADD), and Ralph Nader, who knows so much about lobbying for many causes. Fleischer's basic premise is that teachers are very much like community organizers and social activists in that they all "stress the importance of building a community . . . try to develop leaders . . . reject complacency . . . [and] use organizing skills every day . . ." (p. 118). The big difference between teachers and organizers and activists is that teachers tend not to go public. Fleischer believes that literacy is "everybody's business" (from the title of her book), and that it is teachers' responsibility to make their practices known so that families can and will advocate for those practices. She is committed to the idea that teachers must see their jobs "through the lens of community organization" (p. 50) so that the public understands what teachers are doing and why.

Fleischer offers many strategies for organizing community outreach. She offers ideas about parent study groups, family newsletters, dealing with the media, and other forums for informing the public about students' learning and teachers' practices. She suggests ways in which teachers can write letters to editors and legislators. She also presents information on meeting with legislators, even if those meetings are brief. She helped me imagine a brief meeting with a legislator in which a teacher deposits hundreds of letters of support on the legislator's desk (with media coverage, if possible) as a powerful way for teachers to engage as activists.

Fleischer reminds teachers not to act alone and to remember that they will be teaching at their school for a while. This means that we need to consider the impacts and ramifications of our actions carefully. But Fleischer reminds us, if we stay silent, others will paint pictures that publicly represent us. If we don't like those pictures or if we want a say in how we are portrayed, we need to be proactive.

> We teachers are regular people, leading pretty normal lives, but, too often instead of being local heroes, we wait for a mythical somebody to come along and lead the charge. What community organizing teaches me is this: that we—as ordinary and regular as we are—can be that mythical someone.
>
> And the truth is, we've seen what happens when we don't get actively involved, and it is not a pretty sight. We become a character in a story about education that has been authored by somebody else, somebody who doesn't have the knowledge, the experience, or, all too often, the compassion that we have toward all the kids we welcome into our teaching and learning communities. (Fleischer, 2000, p. 192)

Fleischer's book offers many step-by-step strategies that come from a variety of "orientations toward community organizing" (p. 84). This is required reading for those of us who are serious about organizing to maintain teaching as a profession in which thoughtful educators are appreciated for what they can do with their students.

"High Stakes Are for Tomatoes"

Harman's (2000) concern is the high-stakes testing that is occurring in most states. She wrote that "high stakes are for tomatoes" (p. 332), and that it is time for teachers to act on behalf of their students. Harman recommended that teachers use strategies to address high-stakes testing, and these strategies could also be useful in addressing the type of phonics program that Karen is forced to use. Harman wants teachers to become more knowledgeable about authentic assessment. Elaborating on that point, the need is for teachers to become smarter about whatever is threatening their freedom to address their students' needs. Harman suggested that teachers:

> . . . urge unions to stand up to high-stakes testing; write op/ed pieces and letters to local papers; propose resolutions . . . to professional organizations we belong to; hold teach-ins for parents, school board members, and other teachers . . . ; meet with elected state representatives to educate them on the issues; and buy, give, and wear [clothing such as t-shirts that state our position]. (p. 332)

Harman's focus, again, is on standardized tests, but her strategies are relevant to Karen and her colleagues around the country. Harman's strategies are focused on teachers gaining voice and having presence in the discussions that are taking place. This can apply to phonics programs as well as high-stakes standardized tests. Undoubtedly, we will be criticized for the way we teach math, science, social studies, and more in the years ahead. Yet as Gallagher (2000) asked, "when will we question those 'experts' who are questioning us?" (p. 504). He suggested (also about testing, but very relevant to phonics and other prefabricated scripted curriculum):

> The time is right, I think, for teachers K–college to speak and to work publicly and collectively against standardized assessment, against the testing industry, against the corporatization of American schooling and the deprofessionalization of teacher work, and against the American cultural desire to rank and sort students and teachers as if they were commodities. (p. 504)

Quite often those standardized tests result in standardized curriculum that supposedly will raise scores, thus defusing the *problem* of low-scoring children.

Slowing Swift Curriculum Adoptions

It is time to work against any curriculum that treats students and teachers as commodities. Our students are not products that we are manufacturing. Learning is not as simple as some kind of gross input–output formula devised for industry. Our schools should not be run by or like corporations, but there is pressure for that to happen and that pressure realizes itself in programs like the one Karen must use. One response may be to insist that we are more than perfunctory members of curriculum selection committees. When districts move too swiftly to enact curriculum, we need to ask lots of questions and work to inform the public about the risks of the simplistic solutions (one phonics program for all children) proposed by certain groups.

Sometimes the district goal seems to be to create a portrait of teachers as informed professionals who are always included as integral members of curriculum decision-making committees. Too often the decisions do not truly include teachers' voices, but are made to seem so. Our role on such committees is to complicate the issues so that committee members (and the community) are informed about what curriculum can be and what it can do. If we can not be on the committees, then we need to find ways to observe and respond to such committees' activities. We need to ask questions about such committee work.

TEACHERS ARE RESEARCHERS,
RESEARCH CAN MAKE A DIFFERENCE

We can also ask questions about our own practices. One of the most powerful ways in which teachers can act is to be inquirers into their own classrooms. By becoming a teacher researcher, you gather data, systematically analyze it, and present it to audiences of your choosing. This section is a closer look at teacher research as a vehicle for activism.

Teacher researchers know that:

> Every school and every classroom presents its own set of opportunities and constraints and there is no set of practices that is guaranteed of universal success . . .
>
> [They know that] teaching, like learning, is an ongoing process of inquiry, in which the knowledge that is constructed about learners and learning . . . transforms the teacher's way of understanding and acting in the classroom. . . . (Wells, 1999, p. 164)

When teachers take the time and invest the energy to understand their classrooms as researchers, they are different teachers. When our study group (Meyer et al., 1998) decided to be more systematic in our studies of teaching and learning, it changed from reading and discussing to reading, discussing, inquiring, testing, challenging, and more. The teachers became more systematic in their study of specific facets of their lives and their students' lives in schools. We were intrigued, frustrated, joyous, sorrowful, and more. The range of emotions was intense as we considered what we could say we truly knew and understood about students and ourselves. Once the work was done, we knew we had changed, students had changed, relationships with families had changed, and relationships with colleagues had changed. The teachers in our group knew their students better than they had any previous school year. We had explored many of the subtleties of living and learning in schools, and we didn't keep our learning to ourselves.

We knew that we had to share our findings with others because of the urgency that saturated our work. We attended local and national conferences and presented at other elementary schools in the area. The teachers had frequent visitors to their classrooms as word spread that they were engaging in different sorts of teaching based on what we were learning. Families became increasingly curious about what was occurring in the classrooms, and they began to visit before and after school more frequently. The principal was proud of what the teachers were doing, and he told other principals. Eventually, we wrote the book cited earlier, and our group continued to meet for years.

The research that the teachers were doing was political because it influenced their position in the district. They became resources (and threats) to other teachers and administrators. This is political work because the teachers were constructing curriculum with children, and this activity threatened the positions of district curriculum administrators because it could ultimately influence what the district purchased for classroom use. Perhaps this was why Karen and other teachers in the district were told that they were not to create curriculum; they were to deliver it. Perhaps the subtext of this message was that if you, as a teacher, create curriculum, district consultants have to reposition themselves and they don't know what that position might be. In other words, those in power want to maintain the comfort, prestige, and security that comes with power. They don't want to reposition themselves because they think that would mean a loss of their value and prestige in the district. They cannot imagine how they would *control* things if teachers were thinking for themselves.

Teacher researchers know that curriculum control limits children's learning. They know that the control of teachers may give the appearance of a neat and tidy district, but in reality such control means that teaching is not a profession. They know that the control of children's access to knowledge and information that comes with mandated (controlled) curriculum is an offense against humanity because of the ways in which it limits learning and teaching possibilities.

Teacher research is a strategy that makes you smarter and more articulate about life in your classroom. Teachers with whom I work enjoyed reading *Living the Questions* by Hubbard and Power (1999) because it lays out the fundamentals of teacher research in a very accessible fashion. The book suggests that you form a group to study with and begin some research about questions about which you are passionate. I'd suggest finding a professor who will give you credit for your work as well. I say this for selfish reasons. I want to be part of the group of teachers that does this kind of thinking, and I want teachers to accumulate graduate credits that will lead to enhanced salaries and advanced degrees (further evidence of their professional commitments).

Your inquiry should light a fire within. It should come from and enrich passion about your teaching in deeper ways as you spend time studying, particularly if you are studying with others. It is with others that you can cultivate relationships based on whatever knowledge you all bring to the table. You will (hopefully) form a thought collective in which ideas get pooled as data get analyzed.

Teacher research is a new adventure for most teachers. I believe you will find it exciting, and that excitement will overflow to those outside your group as the group makes decisions about audiences for its work. The overflow also makes the work political because it involves making public the uniqueness of your classroom and school. Such public displays of uniqueness (and child and teacher knowledge construction) threaten those who want standardized curriculum with standardized results for standardized teachers and standardized children.

It's important to consider the politics of your research as you initiate and follow through on it. Make decisions about how you might use your findings to enhance the view that others have of you, your students, and teaching in general. You might present your findings to parents, the school board, and other decision makers and stakeholders.

Your students can also be researchers with you. Then they might participate in presentations that you give to others. Tami Filbrant's (1999) sixth-grade students studied their identities and their roots and eventually presented their work to university classes, at local soup kitchens, in a National Council of Teachers of English journal, and in other forums as well. This work transformed their teacher, her students, and family and community members. This changed Tami's position in the district. She, as a teacher and thinker, can now decide how she might use that changed position to influence what she wants to happen in her classroom. She has collected the real stories of children's lives in schools that can make the difference beyond the local arena.

I put a lot of hope in teacher researchers. I hope that they form affiliations in larger forums for greater impact. I hope that they maintain their high energy level and passionate desires to know. I hope that they find others to learn with, including their students and their students' families and the community. I hope that they look ahead for the possibilities and behind for the lessons to be learned there.

HISTORY HAS LESSONS FOR US

For many teachers, the feeling at present is reminiscent of the citizens in "David and Goliath" or other tales of large, strong, and powerful forces dominating the weak. We are looking for some "David" or "Davida" to appear and rescue us (and surprise us). It's not going to happen that way. We are the Davids and Davidas. It is our coming together and ending our isolation and our view of ourselves as victims that will change things.

It was systematic meetings, the opening of forums in which stories could be told and issues could be discussed, that led to the civil rights movement in the 1960s and the union movements of the 1920s and 1930s (Horton, with Kohl & Kohl, 1998). Union movements were involved in changing the lives of child laborers, miners, and others whose lives were endangered at their jobs daily. The civil rights movement led to desegregation and other civil rights legislation and adjudication. The women's movements changed the position of women in the legislature, the economy, politics, communities, and within virtually every discipline of study. Although these movements may seem recent, they have historical roots that led to them and historical ideas and ideals that supported them. They also had many activists willing to dream and share their dreams.

Each of these movements is about the ending of being silenced—the ending of a monologue that claims to speak for all but does not represent all. Martin Luther King, Jr., discussed in Mott (1975), said that, "Too long has our beloved Southland been bogged down in the tragic attempt to live in monologue rather than dialogue" (p. 416). King wrote this from the Birmingham jail, and it is evidence, Mott suggested, that King understood how to use words, his own culture, and his sense of the possibility of changing positions to move others to act peacefully and for greater justice and equity. Perhaps in study groups, teachers might read about Martin Luther King's coming to be heard, or study the women's movement, progressive education, or the ways unions gained (and some teachers might argue lost) strength. Or they might study other countries in which change was brought about by informing and acting in nonviolent ways (Ghandi, 1958). Or study local politics. There are lessons in history from which we can learn and be energized. Greene (1995) called for a return to the zeal that was felt during the 1960s:

> . . . it may be the recovery of imagination that lessens the social paralysis we see around us and restores the sense that something can be done in the name of what is decent and humane. (p. 34)

> We need . . . to recapture some of the experiences of coming together that occurred in the peace movement and the civil rights movement. We need to articulate what it signifies for some of us to support people with AIDS, to feed and house homeless persons in some dignified way, to offer day-long support to the very young in store-front schools, to bring into being teacher communities in our working spaces. (p. 197)

Teachers getting together to think about, read about, and discuss ways in which power and positioning influence their lives is the kind of imaginative work for which Greene is calling. Studying the past and looking toward the possibilities for our students' lives could lead to action that is specific to the situations that students and teachers face as well as contributing to the greater good of democracy. It is this kind of study and discussion that is summed up effectively in that bumper sticker that reads, "Think Globally, Act Locally."

COLLEGES AND UNIVERSITIES

When I began teaching graduate courses at a university, I often heard teachers express the loneliness and isolation that I discussed earlier. They argued that the university was not doing enough to support them. I tended to agree. It seems that as I began my career, I found myself advocating for action *by* teachers, but was not acting *with* them or *for* them beyond my lip service. Well, that changed. Although my primary area of interest was and is young children's literacy lives, I found I could not study that without being in classrooms and living with teachers in the political climates of classrooms and schools. Part of being a literacy researcher and a teacher educator has evolved into being a partner with teachers and community members to work together toward a view of teaching as a profession. The reading research community is working toward that partnerships as well, although it is clear that viewing teachers as thoughtful professionals is still far from the norm:

> The responsibility within the reading research community is clear: Plan for a program of research that informs the practice of teacher education but also informs the public regarding the benefits of such a deliberate, reflective approach. (Hoffman & Pearson, 2000, p. 41)

Hollingsworth (1992) wrote about the shift in her thinking as a university professor:

> Politically, the move to the conversational format for support and research involved a shift in power from my previous role as the teachers' course instructor. I had to change my interactions so that I was no longer telling teachers what I knew (as the group's "expert" on the topic of reading instruction) and checking to see if they had learned it. I had to develop a process of working with them as a co-learner and creator of evolving expertise

through non-evaluative conversations. To accomplish this, I had to be still and listen. I also had to struggle publicly with what I was learning. Our change in relationship now required that I look at transformation in my own learning . . . as equally important in determining the success of teachers' knowledge transformations. (p. 375)

Hollingsworth (1994) described the intense meetings that she had with new teachers as they worked to make sense of their practice. Her work and the works of other inspired me to develop a new term. Rather than work *on* teachers during inservices (and in courses), I now refer to my work *with* and for teachers as "servicing-in" (Meyer, 1995). This means that I build agendas for study with teachers based on their expressed needs in their school and community contexts. I like to think that this approach is more democratic. I also got tired of feeling like a talking head or a performer when asked to do inservices. Instead, I prefer to work in longer termed, more sustained relationships to help **us** learn new things to enhance students' learning. This means that sometimes I am the expert and sometimes others who attend the servicing-in (or course) are experts.

Practicing teachers are considered to be consumers in the eyes of universities that offer advanced degrees in education. Teachers can demand more of what we want or need from the university, including workshops and other forums in which we can address what we need. Some universities have structures that allow newer courses to be tried on as workshops so these experiences can get "on the books" with little red tape.

What else do you want from your local university or colleges of education? How can you work to make them a place where you not only get credit for an experience, but also learn what you need to know to cultivate teaching as a profession? How can (should) that university or college serve you and your students better? These institutions are a wonderful potential resource. We need to work with them to help realize some of the possibilities that reside within that potential.

If you work as a cooperating teacher with preservice teachers, you have an important opportunity to influence thinking. Like Willis and Harris (2000), you and I, as we work with future teachers, can be "committed to helping our students develop socially just literacy learning spaces for all children" (p. 76). Universities and colleges should be helping inservice and preservice teachers assess curriculum for how well it "accept[s] the children, their culture, their language, and their ways of knowing into the literacy classroom" (p. 81). A cooperating teacher is an important link between the elementary school and the university or college. When a cooperating teacher shares ideas like those in this book with a student teacher, that cooperating teacher is engaging in important political work. Karen had these discussions with her student teacher. Our work with future teachers is conscious political work when we engage in it as a consciousness raising activity (Freire's, 1970a, "conscientization").

PROFESSIONAL ORGANIZATIONS/
INFORMATION SOURCES

You can also find ideas of ways in which you can organize and act within some of the professional organizations that have historically dealt with issues of reading.

The Whole Language Umbrella

For the past 3 years, the annual WLU conference offered preconvention workshops on teaching, politics, and activism. This annual conference occurs near the end of July and the beginning of August. For more information about the preconference in particular, as well as sessions during the conference at which teachers tell stories of their struggles and actions, refer to the Web site of the National Council of Teachers of English (NCTE; ncte.org). NCTE now administrates the Whole Language Umbrella; that is why they are both accessible from the same Web site.

National Council of Teachers of English

The National Council of Teachers of English recently published (available first at their annual convention in Nashville, November 1998) a strategy packet for teachers interested in writing to various commissions, legislators, and more. The packet includes addresses, e-mail addresses, and phone numbers of congress people. It also lists various committees on which legislators serve and sample letters to write to those individuals.

Karen Smith, the NCTE person responsible for bringing the packet together, also included "Fact Sheets" in the strategy pack. Fact Sheets are one- or two-page responses to reading and writing issues in language that could inform the public. Fact Sheets topics include: spelling, beginning reading, bilingual programs, and more. There were 10 Fact Sheets in the packet, and more are being written. Teachers are encouraged to duplicate the Fact Sheets as part of informing the public about what should happen in schools.

In chapter 8, I discussed how an uninformed press can hurt us. Ladson-Billings (1994) described the impact more poignantly:

> Literacy can be a tool of liberation, but, equally, it can be a means of control: if the presses are controlled by the adversaries of a community, then reading can serve as a tool of indoctrination. (p. 94)

Sometimes the press is an adversary of the local community and school. It falls to us to respond to their position so that the public is not indoctrinated as foes of public education. The Fact Sheets can help in that they are ready to be sent to local newspapers, families, and others who might benefit from reading them.

The strategy packet also includes sample letters to editors of local newspapers so that teachers can get an idea of ways to respond to some of the negative press that schools face. The strategy packet helps teachers engage in public relations at the local level so that the criticisms of our teaching are not the only impressions the public has. NCTE also has a political arm that has historically dealt with issues of censorship. This is also accessible on the Web site by clicking on "SLATE."

Many Levels of Conferences

Both NCTE and IRA have local, state, regional, and national conferences. Attend these conferences as a place to find other colleagues to support you in your activism. Also consider proposing sessions at these conferences so that you can voice what you are feeling, both within your session and vicariously through the organization as it accepts proposals from teachers who want to tell their stories and engage in political activity. The more proposals that flood these organizations, the more they will pay attention to the content and focus of those sessions. Proposing a session is like casting a ballot for your beliefs. These organizations also publish a wide variety of books to help us keep informed.

A Lobbyist

The International Reading Association (IRA) has a lobbyist named Richard Long. He reports on his work in *Reading Today*, one of the IRA's journals. You can write to him or visit IRA at ira.org on the web. IRA has worked with NCTE to develop standards (National Council of Teachers of English/International Reading Association, 1996) that may be useful to teachers and others wishing to demonstrate ways that children learn. Do not implicitly trust any organization. Be a critical reader and see if what the organization presents is a representation of your stances and beliefs. Just as we don't want our teaching scripted by a distant author, we don't want our views scripted by an organization. Be as critical a reader as you want your students to be.

Fairtest

Fairtest is a very well-organized group that has responded to the current high-stakes testing madness in the United States. You can read more at: <http://www.fairtest.org/>. Following links from this site will take you to many interesting and supportive sites.

When It's Your Turn to Present

There may come a time when you have the opportunity to present to a group that is not informed about the teaching and learning of reading (and writing). One book that may help is *Creating Support for Effective Literacy Education: Workshop Materials and Handouts* (Weaver, Gillmeister-Krause, & Vento-Zogby, 1996). It explains reading and writing development through the use of blackline masters that teachers can make into overheads. The masters are accompanied by text in which the authors explain how to use the overheads with families, community members, and others. There are also brochures that can be reproduced and distributed that explain issues relevant to reading and writing development. This book is a must have. I've used it to orient families to ways of teaching and learning reading and writing. I used some of the overheads at a session of the state legislator's committee on education and in other local forums in which I am becoming somewhat present. This book is a good resource, but there are no silver bullets, no quick fixes. There are locally crafted and well-informed actions that books like this help serve.

There are too many Web sites, books, and informational pieces to name them all here. The important thing is to get smarter and trust what you've learned from your years as a teacher. There are ideas in the many references I've cited, **and** you have to invent local strategies to address local needs (just like teachers do in their work with children).

IT'S TIME

Karen knows that it is time to act. She spoke to me, invited me to her class-room, and inspired this book. She is thinking about ways to make phonics lessons brief and specific to her students' needs while maintaining a front to present as long as there are phonics patrols checking up on her. She is talking to colleagues and watching state politics closely. She is deciding which professional national convention will be the best forum for her continued learning. She is telling the stories of phonics lessons in her class-rooms to her principal and discussing the stories with colleagues. She is changing her teaching identity to include activism.

It is time for us to talk to each other. It is time because talking to each other gives us access to "the inner ground from which good teaching comes and to the community of fellow teachers from whom we can learn more about ourselves and our craft" (Palmer, 1998, p. 45). Action might or might not originate in the forums of graduate courses, professional conferences, or other places that seem to generate one-time discussion but little activity. If one place does not help us, we need to keep looking.

It is time for us to use our imaginations, as Maxine Greene suggested, to imagine schools and classrooms in which professional teachers are encouraged to use their knowledge of pedagogy and literacy to support children's learning. Our classrooms need to be language *exploratoriums* (a name I borrow from the wonderful interactive learning environment in California) in which local languages, knowledges, and interests are the basis for teaching. It is time for teachers to reappropriate (or appropriate for the first time) reading curriculum, thus engaging in the political activities of teaching and curriculum co-construction with students, families, and the communities in which they work. Vito Perrone (1991) has a sense for what might happen as teachers become activists who advocate for their students and the profession:

> . . . if we saw the development of active inquirers as a major goal [of schools], much that now exits—workbooks and textbooks, predetermined curriculum, reductionism, teaching to tests—would, I believe, begin to fade. (p. 9)

What would flourish and bloom in their place would be relevant and educative teaching and learning experiences at the hands of professional teachers.

IS THE ENEMY US?

One of the most difficult things to do is to change some fundamental part of who we are—to alter our identities. I know that for many teachers, this book is making that sort of request. I am calling for a shift in who we are, what we believe we're supposed to do, and how we might spend our time and limited energy.

Ira Shor (Shor & Freire, 1987) wrote that, "I do find a 'culture of silence' in my mainstream American classrooms. . . . One element is the students' internalizing of passive roles scripted for them in the traditional classroom" (p. 122). Many of the preservice teachers in my classes are the individuals who loved school, prospered there, and even went home and played school (because they couldn't get enough of it during school!). This isn't a "bad" thing. It shows that those individuals were happy in school, they fit there, and their identities were safe there. Part of that identity included compliance to teachers' wishes and demands. Now we can see that, whereas some played school, others dreaded it. Knowing that some are so hurt by school is consciousness that calls for action. Just what it is that you decide to do must involve you being truthful to who you are, to your identity as a teacher, and your understanding of what it means to be with and for children as a professional. Perhaps these words will offer you some of the support and inspiration I've found in them:

> I have been warned and threatened, but somehow I have persisted in holding onto my beliefs and values. I have continued to discover ways to significant growth for myself and support of others. At times only my own will, and my own strength, courage, and knowledge, affirmed me and enabled me to continue to live in situations of intense attack aimed at bringing about my conformity or reducing me to passive silence. (Moustakas, 1995, p. 12)

Teaching has changed. For many of us, this is no easy realization, but one that is borne of curriculum mandate and demanding of action. We must understand and be willing to make public our beliefs and values. We must continue to "discover ways of significant growth," and we must support others in their growth to avoid *conformity* or be *reduced to passive silence*.

AND, IN THE END . . .

In times of intense attack aimed at bringing about student and teacher conformity, we cannot remain silent. The cost is too high. For those of us who went into teaching because of our quiet and conforming nature, I'm sorry.

I'm sorry for how difficult it may be to face the ideas that I've presented here. But I am not sorry that I am asking that we act because our actions will lead us to understand that the teaching of phonics in systematic, intense, direct instruction programs to all children is much more than the teaching of the sounds that letters make.

Teaching phonics this way is a slow process that chips away at authentic and relevant teaching and learning, displaces individuality by demanding sameness, and grates at the fiber of children's definition of reading and their literacy identities. Our responses to such programs are manifested in our teaching, talking, relationships, knowledge base, experiences, and actions. This book, then, is a call to action. It is a call to let others know what you know, why you know it, and how you teach from it. It is a call to save the uniqueness of the learning environment that you develop each year with your students, an environment that celebrates all of the richness that they bring to your classroom.

Just as your children's learning is at stake, your teaching identity is on the line, and your actions at the local level may make huge differences in what you can do in your classroom. The academic freedom that we've come to love in our democracy is at stake, and all of us, as unaccustomed to social action as we might be, are deeply involved. Everything we do or don't do makes a difference. If this feels like a huge weight, that's because it is. Our future is up to our actions.

YOUR THOUGHTS

What's next for you? With whom will you enact what you are thinking? Where will you find support? The next story is yours, the one that you will tell. . . .

Appendix:
Maybe Rules Are Not
the Way to Teach Phonics

This appendix is based on information in chapter 3. Read that chapter first to get the most out of this exercise. It is based on Clymer (1996).

In this appendix, my goal is to help you make decisions about what "rules" to teach to students who are learning to read. Our teaching decisions are based on our assumptions about language. This quiz may help you examine those assumptions. Before you begin, decide about the reliability you want a phonics "rule" to have:

> Make a commitment before you read any of the following items. Decide *right now* what percentage of utility you want a phonics "rule" to have before you would teach it to children who are beginning readers. Write that number in the box.

The number in the box is your criteria; you'd want a rule to work at least that often before you'd teach it. The number in the box is your "guesstimate of reliability of the generalization."

For each item, write a word that fits the generalization; if you can, think of a word to write that does not fit the generalization. Then on the line after the item, write the percentage of words in which you think the generalization works. Finally, based on the percentage you wrote and other factors you consider as a teacher, decide whether you would teach this generalization, how, and when.

Note.   Letter(s) enclosed in / / refer to the sound of the letter. Those enclosed in < > refer to the letter name.

I'll do the first one for you in a number of ways. First, look at Item 1,
then look at Items 1a and 1b to see two possible ways of responding. Let's
suppose I'm like Clymer (1996) and I put a 75 in the box because I want a
rule to work 75% of the time before I'd call it reliable. Your number might
be higher or lower; it's up to you.

1. When there are two vowels side by side, the long sound of the first
one is heard and the second is usually silent.

_____ works for this generalization; _____ does not.

"Guesstimate" of reliability of the generalization: _____%

Would you teach it?_____

One response might be this:
1a. When there are two vowels side by side, the long sound of the first
one is heard and the second is usually silent.
Bean works for this generalization; *great* does not.
"Guesstimate" of reliability of the generalization: *80%*
Would you teach it? *Yes (because the 80% of times that I think it works is
greater than my cutoff mark of 75%).*
Or, look at it this way . . .
1b. When there are two vowels side by side, the long sound of the first
one is heard and the second is usually silent.
Boat works for this generalization; *book* does not.
"Guesstimate" of reliability of the generalization: *65%*
Would you teach it? *No (because the 65% utility rate is less than my 75%
cutoff criteria).*

*Now do the rest without my help. Clymer's results are at the end of the
quiz. I did not keep separate the 45 generalizations that he found because
it makes the quiz too long. I've combined some to get this down to 35
items.*

2. When a vowel is in the middle of a one-syllable word, the vowel is short.

_____ works for this generalization; _____ does not.

"Guesstimate" of reliability of the generalization: _____%

Would you teach it?_____

3. If the only vowel is at the end of a word, the letter usually stands for a long sound.

_____works for this generalization; _____ does not.

"Guesstimate" of reliability of the generalization: _____%

Would you teach it?_____

4. When there are two vowels in a word, one of which is final <e>, and the vowels are separated by a consonant, the first vowel is long and the <e> is silent.

_____works for this generalization; _____ does not.

"Guesstimate" of reliability of the generalization: _____%

Would you teach it?_____

5. An <r> gives the preceding vowel a sound that is neither long nor short.

_____works for this generalization; _____ does not.

"Guesstimate" of reliability of the generalization: _____%

Would you teach it?_____

6. When the letter <i> is followed by the letters <gh>, the <i> usually stands for its long sound and the <gh> is silent.

_____works for this generalization; _____ does not.
"Guesstimate" of reliability of the generalization: _____%

Would you teach it?_____

7. When <a> follows <w> in a word, it usually has the sound of /ŭ/ in *was*.

_____ works for this generalization; _____ does not.

"Guesstimate" of reliability of the generalization: _____%

Would you teach it? _____
Note. Clymer did not study this one. I've added it in for more fun!

8. The two letters <o> and <w> make the long /o/ sound.

_____ works for this generalization; _____ does not.

"Guesstimate" of reliability of the generalization: _____%

Would you teach it? _____

9. <W> is sometimes a vowel and follows the vowel digraph rule. (Bonus credit for answer: What is the vowel digraph rule? When is <w> a vowel?)

_____ works for this generalization; _____ does not.

"Guesstimate" of reliability of the generalization: _____%

Would you teach it? _____

10. When <y> is the final letter in a word, it usually has a vowel sound. (See the following item, too.)

_____ works for this generalization; _____ does not.

"Guesstimate" of reliability of the generalization: _____%

Would you teach it? _____

11. When <y> is used as a vowel in words, it sometimes has the sound of long /ī/. (Bonus question: What's the rule for when it sounds like /ī/ or /ē/ or ??)

_____ works for this generalization; _____ does not.

"Guesstimate" of reliability of the generalization: _____%

Would you teach it?_____

12. The letter <a> has the same sound (/ŏ/) when followed by <l>, <w>, and <u>.

_____works for this generalization; _____ does not.

"Guesstimate" of reliability of the generalization: _____%

Would you teach it?_____

13. When <a> is followed by <r> and final <e>, we expect to hear the sound heard in *care*.

_____works for this generalization; _____ does not.

"Guesstimate" of reliability of the generalization: _____%

Would you teach it?_____

14. When <c> and <h> are next to each other, they make only one sound. (Bonus question: What is the name some linguists use for the sound?)

_____works for this generalization; _____ does not.

"Guesstimate" of reliability of the generalization: _____%

Would you teach it?_____

15. When <c> is followed by <e> or <i>, the sound of /s/ is likely to be heard.

_____works for this generalization; _____ does not.

"Guesstimate" of reliability of the generalization: _____%

Would you teach it?_____

16. When <c> is followed by <o> or <a>, the sound of /k/ is likely to be heard.

_____works for this generalization; _____ does not.

"Guesstimate" of reliability of the generalization: _____%

Would you teach it?_____

17. The letter <g> often has a sound similar to that of <j> in *jump* when it precedes the letter <i> or <e>.
_____works for this generalization; _____ does not.

"Guesstimate" of reliability of the generalization: _____%

Would you teach it?_____

18. When <ght> is seen in a word, <gh> is silent.

_____works for this generalization; _____ does not.

"Guesstimate" of reliability of the generalization: _____%

Would you teach it?_____

19. When a word begins with <kn>, the <k> is silent.

_____works for this generalization; _____ does not.

"Guesstimate" of reliability of the generalization: _____%

Would you teach it?_____

20. When a word begins with <wr>, the <w> is silent.

_____works for this generalization; _____ does not.

"Guesstimate" of reliability of the generalization: _____%

Would you teach it?_____

21. When two of the same consonants are side by side, only one is heard.

_____works for this generalization; _____ does not.

"Guesstimate" of reliability of the generalization: _____%

Would you teach it?_____

22. When a word ends in <ck>, it has the same last sound as in *look*. (Can you see why kids write "loock" or "sik"?)

_____works for this generalization; _____ does not.

"Guesstimate" of reliability of the generalization: _____%

Would you teach it?_____

23. In most two-syllable words, the first syllable is accented.

_____works for this generalization; _____ does not.

"Guesstimate" of reliability of the generalization: _____%

Would you teach it?_____

24. If <a>, <in>, <re>, <ex>, <de>, or <be> is the first syllable in a word, it is usually unaccented.

_____works for this generalization; _____ does not.

"Guesstimate" of reliability of the generalization: _____%

Would you teach it?_____

25. In most two-syllable words that end in a consonant followed by <y>, the first syllable is accented and the last is unaccented.

_____works for this generalization; _____ does not.

"Guesstimate" of reliability of the generalization: _____%

Would you teach it?_____

26. One vowel in an accented syllable has its short sound.

_____works for this generalization; _____ does not.

"Guesstimate" of reliability of the generalization: _____%

Would you teach it?_____

27. When <ture> is the final syllable in a word, it is unaccented.

_____works for this generalization; _____ does not.

"Guesstimate" of reliability of the generalization: _____%

Would you teach it?_____

28. When <tion> is the final syllable in a word, it is unaccented.

_____works for this generalization; _____ does not.

"Guesstimate" of reliability of the generalization: _____%

Would you teach it?_____

29. If the last syllable of a word ends with <le>, the consonant preceding the <le> usually begins the last syllable.

_____works for this generalization; _____ does not.

"Guesstimate" of reliability of the generalization: _____%

Would you teach it?_____

30. When the first vowel element in a word is followed by <th>, <ch>, or <sh>, these symbols are not broken when the word is divided into syllables and may go with either the first or second syllables.

_____works for this generalization; _____ does not.

"Guesstimate" of reliability of the generalization: _____%

Would you teach it?_____

31. When a word has only one vowel, the vowel sound is likely to be short.

_____works for this generalization; _____ does not.

"Guesstimate" of reliability of the generalization: _____%

Would you teach it?_____

32. When <e> is followed by <w>, the vowel sound is the same as /ü/ in *moon*.

_____works for this generalization; _____ does not.

"Guesstimate" of reliability of the generalization: _____%

Would you teach it?_____

Ready for Clymer's results? Here they are. Next to each number is the percent of times that the rule or generalization worked in the basal that Clymer studied. I also include some of the sample words he reported (Clymer, 1996). He did this work originally in the 1960s when he was teaching and a child asked him why they had to study so many rules when they were so unreliable. Are you asking yourself the same question? Maybe "rules" are not the way to teach phonics (see Moustafa, 1997).

1. When there are two vowels side by side, the long sound of the first one is heard and the second is usually silent.
Bead works for this generalization; *chief* does not.
Reliability of the generalization in the basal[1]: 45%.
2. When a vowel is in the middle of a one-syllable word, the vowel is short.
Dress, *rest*, *splash* work for this generalization; *told* and *fight* do not.
Reliability of the generalization in the basal: 62%.
3. If the only vowel is at the end of a word, the letter usually stands for a long sound.
He works for this generalization; *to* does not.
Reliability of the generalization in the basal: 74%.

[1]These numbers refer to the words Clymer analyzed in the specific basal he considered in his research. It does not mean for all basal reading systems.

4. When there are two vowels, one of which is final <e>, the first vowel is long and the <e> is silent.
Bone works for this generalization; *done* does not.
Reliability of the generalization in the basal: <u>63%</u>.

5. The <r> gives the preceding vowel a sound that is neither long nor short.
Horn works for this generalization; *wire* does not.
Reliability of the generalization in the basal: <u>78%</u>.

6. When the letter <i> is followed by the letters <gh>, the <i> usually stands for its long sound and the <gh> is silent.
High works for this generalization; *neighbor* does not.
Reliability of the generalization in the basal: <u>71%</u>.

7. When <a> follows <w> in a word, it usually has the sound of /ŭ/ in *was*.
Watch works for this generalization; *swan* does not.
Note. Clymer did not study this one. How often do you see it working?

8. The two letters <o> and <w> make the long /ō/ sound.
Own works for this generalization; *down* does not.
Reliability of the generalization in the basal: <u>59%</u>.

9. <W> is sometimes a vowel and follows the vowel digraph rule. (Bonus credit for answer: What is the vowel digraph rule? When is <w> a vowel?)
Crow works for this generalization; *threw* does not.
Reliability of the generalization in the basal: <u>40%</u>.
Bonus answer: When <w> works with a vowel to make the sound of a vowel or vowels, it is a vowel. (<W> is a vowel in *now* and *snow*.) The digraph rule says the first vowel will be long.

10. When <y> is the final letter in a word, it usually has a vowel sound. (See the following item too.)
Dry works for this generalization; *tray* does not.
Reliability of the generalization in the basal: <u>84%</u>.

11. When <y> is used as a vowel in words, it sometimes has the sound of long /ī/. (Bonus question: What's the rule for when it sounds like /ī/ or /ē/ or ??)
Fly works for this generalization; *funny* does not.
Reliability of the generalization in the basal: <u>84%</u>.
(Bonus answer: <Y> sounds like /ī/ in many one-syllable words (*try*) and like /ē/ in two-syllable words (*happy*).

12. The letter <a> has the same sound (dotted /ö/ sound) when followed by <l>, <w>, and <u>.
All works for this generalization; *canal* does not.
Reliability of the generalization in the basal: 48%.

13. When <a> is followed by <r> and final <e>, we expect to hear the sound heard in *care*.
Dare works for this generalization; *are* does not.
Reliability of the generalization in the basal: 48%.

14. When <c> and <h> are next to each other, they make only one sound. (Bonus: What is the name some linguists use for the sound?)
Peach works for this generalization; [*none were found*] does not.
Reliability of the generalization in the basal: 100%.
Bonus answer: Consonant digraph.

15. When <c> is followed by <e> or <i>, the sound of /s/ is likely to be heard.
Cent works for this generalization; *ocean* does not.
Reliability of the generalization in the basal: 96%.

16. When <c> is followed by <o> or <a>, the sound of /k/ is likely to be heard.
Camp works for this generalization; [*none were found*] does not.
Reliability of the generalization in the basal: 100%.

17. The letter <g> often has a sound similar to that of <j> in *jump* when it precedes the letter <i> or <e>.
Engine works for this generalization; *give* does not.
Reliability of the generalization in the basal: 64%.

18. When <ght> is seen in a word, <gh> is silent.
Fight works for this generalization; [*none were found*] does not.
Reliability of the generalization in the basal: 100%.

19. When a word begins with <kn>, the <k> is silent.
Knife works for this generalization; [*none were found*] does not.
Reliability of the generalization in the basal: 100%.

20. When a word begins with <wr>, the <w> is silent.
Write works for this generalization; [*none were found*] does not.
Reliability of the generalization in the basal: 100%.

21. When two of the same consonants are side by side, only one is heard.
Carry works for this generalization; *suggest* does not.
Reliability of the generalization in the basal: 99%.

22. When a word ends in <ck>, it has the same last sound as in *look*. (Can you see why kids write "loock" or "sik"?)
Brick works for this generalization; [*none were found*] does not.
Reliability of the generalization in the basal: 100%.

23. In most two-syllable words, the first syllable is accented.
Famous works for this generalization; *polite* does not.
Reliability of the generalization in the basal: 85%.

24. If <a>, <in>, <re>, <ex>, <de>, or <be> is the first syllable in a word, it is usually unaccented.
Belong works for this generalization; *insect* does not.
Reliability of the generalization in the basal: 87%.

25. In most two-syllable words that end in a consonant followed by <y>, the first syllable is accented and the last is unaccented.
Baby works for this generalization; *supply* does not.
Reliability of the generalization in the basal: 96%.

26. One vowel letter in an accented syllable has its short sound.
City works for this generalization; *lady* does not.
Reliability of the generalization in the basal: 61%.

27. When <ture> is the final syllable in a word, it is unaccented.
Picture works for this generalization; [*none were found*] does not.
Reliability of the generalization in the basal: 100%.

28. When <tion> is the final syllable in a word, it is unaccented.
Station works for this generalization; [*none were found*] does not.
Reliability of the generalization in the basal: 100%.

29. If the last syllable of a word ends with <le>, the consonant preceding the <le> usually begins the last syllable.
Tumble works for this generalization; *buckle* does not.
Reliability of the generalization in the basal: 96%.

30. When the first vowel element in a word is followed by <th>, <ch>, or <sh>, these symbols are not broken when the word is divided into syllables and may go with either the first or second syllables.
Dishes works for this generalization; [*none were found*] does not.
Reliability of the generalization in the basal: 100%.

31. When a word has only one vowel, the vowel sound is likely to be short.
Hid works for this generalization; *kind* does not.
Reliability of the generalization in the basal: 57%.

32. When <e> is followed by <w>, the vowel sound is the same as represented by /ü/ in *moon*.
Blew works for this generalization; *sew* does not.
Reliability of the generalization in the basal: <u>35%</u>.

If you didn't know these rules well enough to state them and think of examples, *and* you can still read, why teach them to children?

References

Adams, M. (1994). *Beginning to read: Thinking and learning about print.* Cambridge, MA: MIT Press.

Allington, R. (1997, August/September). Overselling phonics: Five unscientific assertions about reading instruction. *Reading Today,* pp. 15–16.

Allington, R., & Woodside-Jiron, H. (1998). Thirty years of research in reading: When is a research summary not a research summary. In K. Goodman (Ed.), *In defense of good teaching: What teachers need to know about the reading wars* (pp. 143–157). York, ME: Stenhouse.

Allington, R., & Woodside-Jiron, H. (1999). The politics of literacy teaching: How "research" shaped educational policy. *Educational Researcher, 28*(8), 4–13.

Altwerger, B. (1998). Whole language as decoy: The real agenda behind the attacks. In K. Goodman (Ed.), *In defense of good teaching: What teachers need to know about the "Reading Wars."* (pp. 175–182). York, ME: Stenhouse.

Altwerger, B., & Bird, L. (1982, January). Disabled: the learner or the curriculum? *Topics in Learning Disabilities,* pp. 69–78.

Angelou, M. (1971). How I can lie to you. In *Just give me a cool drink of water 'fore I diiie.* New York: Random House.

Angelou, M. (1992). *Wouldn't trade nothing for my journey now.* New York: Bantam.

Applebee, A. N. (1996). *Curriculum as conversation: Transforming traditions of teaching and learning.* Chicago: University of Chicago Press.

Atwell, N. (1998). *In the middle: Writing, reading, and learning with adolescents.* Portsmouth, NH: Heinemann.

Au, K. (1993). *Literacy instruction in multicultural settings.* Fort Worth, TX: Harcourt Brace Janovich.

Avery, C. (1993). *And with a light touch.* Portsmouth, NH: Heinemann.

Barr, R., Kamil, M., Mosenthal, P., & Pearson, P. D. (Eds.). (1996). *Handbook of reading research: Volume II.* Mahwah, NJ: Lawrence Erlbaum Associates.

Baylor, B. (1992). *Yes is better than no.* Tucson, AZ: Treasure Chest Publications.

Belenky, M., Clinchy, B., Goldberger, N., & Tarule, J. (1986). *Women's ways of knowing: The development of self, voice, and mind.* New York: Basic Books.

Bell, D. (1992). *Faces at the bottom of the well: The permanence of racism.* New York: Basic Books.

Berliner, D. C., & Biddle, B. J. (1995). *The manufactured crisis: Myths, fraud, and the attack on America's public schools.* Reading, MA: Addison-Wesley.

Bever, T. G., & Bower, T. G. (1966, January). *How to read without listening* (Project Literacy Reports No. 6, Educational Resources Information Center, ED 010 312: 13–25).

Bloome, D. (1983). Reading as a social process. *Advances in Reading/Language Research, 2,* 165–195.

Bond, G., & Dykstra, R. (1967/1997). The cooperative research program in first-grade reading instruction. *Reading Research Quarterly, 32,* 348–427.

Brady, J. (1995). *Schooling young children: A feminist pedagogy for liberatory learning.* Albany: SUNY.

Braunger, J., & Lewis, J. (1997, October). *Building a knowledge base in reading.* Urbana, IL: National Council of Teachers of English.

Bredekamp, S. (Ed.). (1987). *Developmentally appropriate practice in early childhood programs serving children from birth through age 8.* Washington, DC: National Association for the Education of Young Children.

Brinkley, E., Weaver, C., Campbell, P., Houston, M., Williams, J., Little, V., Mohaghan, M., Freedman, L., Bird, B., & Bird, J. (1997). Believing in what's possible, taking action to make a difference. *Language Arts, 74*(7), 537–544.

Brown, J., Marek, A., & Goodman, K. S. (1996). *Studies in miscue analysis: An annotated bibliography.* Newark, DE: International Reading Association.

Brueggemann, B. J. (1996). Still-life: Representations and silences in the participant-observer role. In P. Mortensen & G. E. Kirsch (Eds.), *Ethics and representation in qualitative studies of literacy* (pp. 17–39). Urbana, IL: National Council of Teachers of English.

Cambourne, B. (1995). Toward an educationally relevant theory of literacy learning: Twenty years of inquiry. *Reading Teacher, 49*(3), 182–190.

Cambourne, B. (2000, July). *Politics, literacy education, and democracy.* Paper presented at the annual meeting of the Australia Literacy Educators Association, Melbourne, Australia.

Carbo, M. (1988, November). Debunking the great phonics myth. *Phi Delta Kappan, 71*(2), 226–239.

Carini, P. (1979, September). *The art of seeing and the visibility of the person.* Grand Forks, ND: University of North Dakota.

Cazden, C. (1988). *Classroom discourse: The language of teaching and learning.* Portsmouth, NH: Heinemann.

Chall, J. (1989, March). Learning to read: The great debate 20 years later—A response to "debunking the great phonics myth." *Phi Delta Kappan, 70*(7), 521–537.

Clymer, T. (1996). The utility of phonic generalizations in the primary grades. *Reading Teacher, 50*(3), 182–187.

Cochran, O., Cochran, D., Scalena, S., & Buchanan, E. (1985). *Reading, writing and caring.* Winnipeg, Manitoba: Whole Language Consultants.

Cochran-Smith, M., & Lytle, S. (2000). Relationships of knowledge and practice: Teacher learning in communities. In A. Iran-Nudged & P. D. Pearson (Eds.), *Review of research in education* (Vol. 24, pp. 249–306). Washington, DC: AERA.

Cole, J. (1986). *The magic school bus at the waterworks.* New York: Scholastic.

Coles, G. (2000). *Misreading reading: The bad science that hurts children.* Portsmouth, NH: Heinemann.

Coles, R. (1989). *The call of stories: Teaching and the moral imagination.* Boston: Houghton Mifflin.

Cunninghan, J., & Fitzgerald, J. (1996). Epistemology and reading. *Reading Research Quarterly, 31*(1), 36–60.

Daneman, M. (1996). Individual differences in reading skills. In R. Barr, M. Kamil, P. Mosenthal, & P. D. Pearson (Eds.), *Handbook of reading research: Vol. II* (pp. 512–538). Mahwah, NJ: Lawrence Erlbaum Associates.

Darling-Hammond, L. (1996). The right to learn and the advancement of teaching: Research, policy, and practice for democratic education. *Educational Researcher, 25*(6), 5–17.

Darling-Hammond, L. (2000, February). *Preparing teachers for the 21st century.* Paper presented at the National Council of Teachers of English Assembly for Research Midwinter Conference: Preparing Language Arts Teachers for the 21st Century: Research, Practice, and Policy, Seattle, WA.

Dechant, E. V. (1970). *Improving the teaching of reading* (2nd ed.). Englewood Cliffs, NJ: Prentice-Hall.

Delpit, L. (1995). *Other people's children: Cultural conflict in the classroom.* New York: The New Press.

Dewey, J. (1904). The relation of theory to practice in education. In C. McMurry (Ed.), *The third yearbook of the National society for the Scientific Study of Education* (pp. 9–30). Chicago: University of Chicago Press.

Dewey, J. (1938). *Experience and education.* New York: Collier Books, Macmillan.

Diaz, R., Neal, C., & Amaya-Williams, M. (1990). The social origins of self-regulation. In L. Moll (Ed.), *Vygotsky and education: Instructional implications and applications of socio-historical psychology* (pp. 127–154). Cambridge: Cambridge University Press.

Dickinson, E. (1951). A word is dead when it is said. In T. H. Johnson, (Ed.). *The poems of Emily Dickinson.* Cambridge, MA: Belknap Press of Harvard University Press.

Dressman, M. (1999, July/August/September). On the use and misuse of research evidence: Decoding two states' reading initiatives. *Reading Research Quarterly, 34*(3), 258–285.

Du Bois, W. E. B. (1969). *An ABC of color.* New York: International Publishers.

Duckworth, E. (1987). *The having of wonderful ideas & other essays on teaching & learning.* New York: Teachers College Press.

Durand, V. M. (1990). *Severe behavior problems: A functional communication training approach.* New York: Guilford.

Edelsky, C. (1996). *With literacy and justice for all: Rethinking the social in language and education.* Bristol, PA: Taylor & Francis.

Edelsky, C. (1998). It's a long story—And it's not done yet. In K. Goodman (Ed.), *In defense of good teaching: What teachers need to know about the reading wars* (pp. 39–57). York, ME: Stenhouse.

Ehri, L. (1996). Development of the ability to read words. In R. Barr, M. Kamil, P. Mosenthal, & P. D. Pearson (Eds.), *Handbook of reading research: Vol. II* (pp. 383–417). Mahwah, NJ: Lawrence Erlbaum Associates.

Filbrandt, T. (1999, October). Poetry and transformation. *Primary Voices, 8*(2), 11–18.

Fine, M. (1987). Silencing in public schools. *Language Arts, 64*, 157–174.

Fisher, B. (1998). *Joyful learning: A whole language kindergarten* (2nd ed.). Portsmouth, NH: Heinemann.

Fleischer, C. (2000). *Teachers organizing for change: Making literacy learning everybody's business.* Urbana, IL: National Council of Teachers of English.

Flesch, R. (1955). *Why Johnny can't read and what you can do about it*. New York: Harper & Row.

Flores Dueñas, L. (1997). *Second language reading: Mexican American student voices on reading Mexican American literature*. Unpublished doctoral dissertation, University of Texas at Austin.

Flurkey, A. (1997). *Reading as flow: A linguistic alternative to fluency*. Unpublished doctoral dissertation, University of Arizona, Tucson.

Fox, M. (1993). *Radical reflections: Passionate opinions on teaching, learning, and living*. San Diego: Harcourt Brace.

Fraser, J., & Skolnick, D. (1996). *On their way: Celebrating second graders as the read and write*. Portsmouth, NH: Heinemann.

Freeman, D., & Freeman, B. (1998). California reading: The pendulum swings. In K. Goodman (Ed.), *In defense of good teaching: What teachers need to know about the reading wars* (pp. 73–85). York, ME: Stenhouse.

Freire, P. (1970a, May). The adult literacy process as cultural action for freedom. *Harvard Educational Review, 40*(2), 205–225.

Freire, P. (1970b). *Pedagogy of the oppressed*. New York: Continuum.

Freire, P., & Macedo, D. (1987). *Literacy: Reading the word and the world*. Westport, CT: Bergin & Garvey.

Gallagher, C. (2000). A seat at the table: Teachers reclaiming assessment through rethinking accountability. *Phi Delta Kappan, 81*(7), 502–507.

Gee, J., Hull, G., & Lankshear, C. (1996). *The new work order: Behind the language of the new capitalism*. Boulder, CO: Westview.

Geertz, C. (1973). Thick description: Toward an interpretive theory of culture. In C. Geertz (Ed.), *The interpretation of cultures* (pp. 3–30). New York: Basic Books.

Ghandi, M. (1958). *All men are brothers: Life and thoughts of Mahatma Gandhi as told in his own words*. Paris: UNESCO.

Glaser, B., & Strauss, A. (1967). *The discovery of grounded theory*. Chicago: Aldine.

Goldstein, L. (1999, Fall). The relational zone: The role of caring relationships in the co-construction of mind. *American Educational Research Journal, 36*(3), 647–673.

Goldstein, L. S. (1998). More than gentle smiles and warm hugs: Applying the ethic of care to early childhood education. *Journal of Research in Childhood Education, 12*(2), 244–261.

Goodman, K. (1967). Reading, a psycholinguistic guessing game. *Journal of the Reading Specialist, 6*, 126–135.

Goodman, K. (1993). *Phonics phacts: A common-sense look at the most controversial issue affecting today's classrooms!* Portsmouth, NH: Heinemann.

Goodman, K. (1996). *On reading: A common-sense look at the nature of language and the science of reading*. Portsmouth, NH: Heinemann.

Goodman, K. (Ed.). (1998). *In defense of good teaching: What teachers need to know about the reading wars*. York, ME: Stenhouse.

Goodman, K., Shannon, P., Freeman, Y., & Murphy, S. (1988). *Report card on the basal readers*. Katonah, NY: Richard C. Owen.

Goodman, Y. (1985). Kidwatching: Observing children in the classroom. In A. Jaggar & M. T. Smith-Burke (Eds.), *Observing the language learner* (pp. 9–18). Urbana, IL: NCTE.

Goodman, Y. (1999, December). *Decodable text is not predictable and it's not decodable either.* Paper presented at the annual meeting of the National Reading Conference, Orlando, FL.

Goodman, Y., Watson, D., & Burke, C. (1987). *Reading miscue inventory: Alternative procedures.* New York: Richard C. Owen.

Graves, D., & Sunstein, B. (1993). *Portfolio portraits.* Portsmouth, NH: Heinemann.

Greene, M. (1995). *Releasing the imagination: Essays on education, the arts, and social change.* San Francisco: Jossey-Bass.

Grossen, B. (1997). *Thirty years of research: What we now know about how children learn to read—A synthesis of research on reading from the National Institute of Child Health and Development.* Santa Cruz, CA: Center for the Future of Teaching and Learning. (www.cftl.org)

Guba, E., & Lincoln, Y. (1982). Epistemological and methodological bases of naturalistic inquiry. *ECTJ, 30*(4), 233–252.

Halliday, M. A. K. (1988). "There's still a long way to go. . . ." An interview with emeritus professor Michael Halliday. *Journal of the Australian Advisory Council on Languages and Multicultural Education,* 35–39.

Halliday, M.A.K., & Hasan, R. (1989). *Language, context, and text: Aspects of language in a social-semiotic perspective.* Oxford: Oxford University Press.

Hallifax, J. (2000, March 15). Florida judge tosses school voucher law. *Albuquerque Journal,* p. A9.

Hanson, G. (1992). *My thinking chair: Daydreams in the lives of children.* Unpublished doctoral dissertation, University of Arizona.

Harman, S. (2000). Resist high stakes testing: High stakes are for tomatoes. *Language Arts, 77*(4), 332.

Healy, J. (1990). *Endangered minds: Why our children don't think.* New York: Simon & Schuster.

Heath, S. B. (1983). *Ways with word: Language, life, and work in communities and classrooms.* New York: Cambridge University Press.

Herbart, J. (1895). The science of education: Its general principles deduced from its aim. In H. Felkin & E. Felkin (Trans.), *The science of education: Its general principles deduced from its aim* (pp. 67–81). Boston: Heath.

Hindley, J. (1996). *In the company of children.* York, ME: Stenhouse.

Hoffman, J., & Pearson, P. D. (2000). Reading teacher education in the next millennium: What your grandmother's teacher didn't know that your granddaughter's teacher should. *Reading Research Quarterly, 35*(1), 28–44.

Holdaway, D. (1979). *The foundations of literacy.* Sydney: Ashton Scholastic.

Hollingsworth, S. (1992, Summer). Learning to teach through collaborative conversation: A feminist approach. *American Educational Research Journal, 29*(2), 373–404.

Hollingsworth, S. (1994). *Teacher research and urban literacy education: Lessons and conversations in a feminist key.* New York: Teachers College Press.

Hornsby, D., Parry, J., & Sukarna, D. (1992). *Teach on: Teaching strategies for reading and writing workshops.* Portsmouth, NH: Heinemann.

Horton, M., with Kohl, J., & Kohl, H. (1998). *The long haul: An autobiography.* New York: Teachers College Press.

Houle, C. (1961). *The inquiring mind.* Madison: University of Wisconsin Press.

Hubbard, R., & Power, B. (1999). *Living the questions: A guide for teacher-research.* York, ME: Stenhouse.

Johnston, P. (1998). The consequences of the use of standardized testing. In S. Murphy, with P. Shannon, P. Johnston & J. Hansen (Eds.), *Fragile evidence: A critique of reading assessment* (pp. 89–102). Mahwah, NJ: Lawrence Erlbaum Associates.

Keresty, B., O'Leary, S., & Wortley, D. (1998). *You can make a difference: A teacher's guide to political action.* Portsmouth, NH: Heinemann.

Kohl, H. (1991). *I won't learn from you: The role of assent in learning.* Minneapolis, MN: Milkweed.

Kolbe, T. (1999, October). Community investigations: Looking at uncertainty. *Primary Voices, 8*(2), 20–27.

Ladson-Billings, G. (1994). *The dreamkeepers: Successful teachers of African American children.* San Francisco: Jossey-Bass.

Lather, P. (1991). *Getting smart: Feminist research and pedagogy with/in the postmodern.* New York: Routledge.

Lortie, D. (1975). *Schoolteacher: A sociological study.* Chicago: University of Chicago Press.

Lowry, L. (1993). *The giver.* Boston: Houghton Mifflin.

Macedo, D. (2000). The colonialism of the English only movement. *Educational Researcher, 29*(3), 15–24.

Madaus, G. (1999). The influence of testing on the curriculum. In M. Early & K. Rehage (Eds.), *Issues in curriculum: Selected chapters from NSSE yearbooks* (pp. 73–111). Chicago: University of Chicago Press.

Martens, P. (1996). *I already know how to read: A child's view of literacy.* Portsmouth, NH: Heinemann.

Martens, P., Flurkey, A., Meyer, R., & Udell, R. (1999). Inventing literacy identities: Intratextual, intertextual, and intercontextual influences on emerging literacy. In T. Shanahan & F. Rodriguez-Brown (Eds.), *99th yearbook of the National Reading Conference* (pp. 73–85). Chicago: NRC.

Martens, P., Goodman, Y., & Flurkey, A. (1995). Special Issue. *Primary Voices, 3*(4).

Martin, B., Jr. (1983). *Brown bear, brown bear, what do you see?* New York: Holt, Rinehart, & Winston.

Martin, B., Jr. (1991). The author interview: An interview by Ralph Fletcher. In N. Atwell (Ed.), *Workshop 3 by and for teachers: The politics of practice* (pp. 132–138). Portsmouth, NH: Heinemann.

Mason, K. (1999, October/November). I've been wondering. *Talking Points, 11*(1), 21–22.

McQuillan, J. (1998). *The literacy crisis: False claims, real solutions.* Portsmouth, NH: Heinemann.

Meek, M. (1988). *How texts teach what readers learn.* South Woodchester, Great Britain: Thimble.

Meier, D. (1995). *The power of their ideas: Lessons for American from a small school in Harlem.* Boston: Beacon.

Meier, D. (1997). *Learning in small moments: Life in an urban classroom.* New York: Teachers College Press.

Meyer, R. (1995). Servicing-in: An approach to teacher and staff development. *Teacher Research, 2*(2), 1–17.

Meyer, R. (1996). *Stories from the heart: Teachers and students researching their literacy lives.* Mahwah, NJ: Lawrence Erlbaum Associates.

Meyer, R., Brown, L., DeNino, E., Larson, K., McKenzie, M., Ridder, K., & Zetterman, K. (1998). *Composing a teacher study group: Learning about inquiry in primary classrooms.* Mahwah, NJ: Lawrence Erlbaum Associates.

Mills, H., O'Keefe, T., & Stephens, D. (1992). *Looking closely: Exploring the role of phonics in one whole language classroom.* Urbana, IL: National Council of Teachers of English.

Moll, L., Veles-Ibanez, C., & Greenberg, J. (1990). *Community knowledge and classroom practice combining resources for literacy instruction: Handbook for teachers and planners from the Innovative Approaches Research Project.* Washington, DC: U.S. Department of Education, Office of Educational Research and Improvement, Educational Resources Information Center.

Mott, W. (1975, December). The rhetoric of Martin Luther King, Jr.: Letter from Birmingham jail. *Phylon, 36*(4), 411–421.

Moustafa, M. (1997). *Beyond traditional phonics: Research discoveries and reading instruction.* Portsmouth, NH: Heinemann.

Moustakas, C. (1995). *Being-in, being-for, being-with.* Northvale, NJ: Jason Aronson.

National Commission on Excellence in Education. (1983). *A nation at risk: The imperative for educational reform: A report to the Nation and the Secretary of Education, United States Department of Education.* Washington, DC: Author.

National Council of Teachers of English/International Reading Association. (1996). *Standards for the English language arts.* Urbana, IL: Author.

Oakes, J. (1985). *Keeping track.* New Haven, CT: Yale University Press.

Ohanian, S. (1999). *One size fits few: The folly of educational standards.* Portsmouth, NH: Heinemann.

Ohanian, S. (2000). Goals 2000: What's in a name? *Phi Delta Kappan, 8*(5), 344–355.

O'Loughlin, M., & Barnes, M. (1999, April). *An inquiry into diverse children's racial formation: Theoretical and critical considerations.* Paper presented at the annual meeting of the American Educational Research Association, Montreal, Canada.

Palmer, P. (1998). *The courage to teach: Exploring the inner landscape of a teacher's life.* San Francisco: Jossey-Bass.

Paris, C. (1993). *Teacher agency and curriculum making in classrooms.* New York: Teachers College Press.

Paris, S., Wasik, B., & Turner, J. (1996). The development of strategic readers. In R. Barr, M. Kamil, P. Mosenthal & P. D. Pearson (Eds.), *Handbook of reading research: Vol. II* (pp. 609–640). Mahwah, NJ: Lawrence Erlbaum Associates.

Paterson, K. (1981). *Gates of excellence: On reading and writing books for children.* New York: Lodestar.

Paul, L. (2000). The naked truth about being literate. *Language Arts, 77*(4), 335–343.

Pearson, P. D. (2000). Panel discussion at the National Council of Teachers of English Assembly for Research Midwinter Conference: Preparing Language Arts Teachers for the 21st Century: Research, Practice, and Policy, Seattle, WA.

Perrone, V. (1991). *A letter to teachers: Reflection on schooling and the art of teaching.* San Francisco: Jossey-Bass.

Perrone, V. (1998). *Teacher with a heart: Reflections on Leonard Covello and community.* New York: Teachers College Press.

Peterson, R., & Eeds, M. (1990). *Grand conversations: Literature groups in action.* New York: Scholastic.

Philips, S. (1971). Participant structures and communicative competence: Warm Springs children in community and classroom. In C. Cazden, V. John, & D. Hymes (Eds.), *Functions of language in the classroom* (pp. 370–393). New York: Teachers College Press.

Pinnell, G. S., & Fountas, I. (1998). *Word matters: Teaching phonics and spelling in the reading/writing classroom* (pp. 370–393). Portsmouth, NH: Heinemann.

Postman, N., & Weingartner, C. (1969). *Teaching as a subversive activity.* New York: Dell.

Putnam, R., & Borko, H. (2000). What do new views of teacher knowledge and thinking have to say about research on teacher learning? *Educational Researcher, 29*(1), 4–15.

Readence, J., & Barone, D. (Eds.). (2000). *Reading Research Quarterly, 35*(1).

Redford, R., & Markey, P. (Producers), & Redford, R. (Director). (1992). *A river runs through it.* [Film]. Burbank: Columbia Tri-Star. Based on the book, *A river runs through it and other stories* by N. Maclean (1976). Chicago: University of Chicago Press.

Rhodes, L. (1981). I had a cat: A language story. *Language Arts, 58,* 773–774.

Richardson, V. (1999). Teacher education and the construction of meaning. In G. Griffin (Ed.), *The education of teachers: 98th yearbook of the national society for the study of education* (pp. 145–166). Chicago: University of Chicago Press.

Richardson, V., Casanova, U., Placier, P., & Guilfoyle, K. (1989). *School children at-risk.* London: Falmer.

Rodriguez, L. (1993). *Always running. La vida loca: Gang days in L.A.* New York: Touchstone.

Roller, K. (1996). *Variability not disability: Struggling readers in a workshop classroom.* Newark, DE: International Reading Association.

Rose, M. (1989). *Lives on the boundary.* New York: Penguin.

Rosenblatt, L. (1978). *The reader, the text, and the poem: The transactional theory of the literary work.* Carbondale and Edwardsville: Southern Illinois University Press.

Routman, R. (1996). *Literacy at the crossroads: Critical talk about reading, writing, and other teaching dilemmas.* Portsmouth, NH: Heinemann.

Shannon, P. (1989). *Broken promises: Reading instruction in the twentieth century.* Granby, MA: Bergin & Garvey.

Shannon, P. (1990). *The struggle to continue: Progressive reading instruction in the United States.* Portsmouth, NH: Heinemann.

Shannon, P. (1995). *Text, lies, & videotape: Stories about life, literacy, & learning.* Portsmouth, NH: Heinemann.

Shor, I., & Freire, P. (1987). *A pedagogy for liberation: Dialogues on transforming education.* Granby, MA: Begin & Garvey.

Short, K. (1999). The search for "balance" in a literature-rich curriculum. *Theory into Practice, 38*(3), 130–137.

Short, K., & Burke, C. (1991). *Creating curriculum: Teachers and students as a community of learners.* Portsmouth, NH: Heinemann.

Sloan, G. D. (1991). *The child as critic: Teaching literature in elementary and middle schools.* New York: Teachers College Press.

Smith, B., Goodman, K., & Meredith, R. (1970). *Language and thinning in the elementary school.* New York: Holt, Rinehart.

Smith, F. (1985). *Reading without nonsense* (2nd ed.). New York: Teachers College Press.

Smith, F. (1988). *Joining the literacy club: Further essays into education.* Portsmouth, NH: Heinemann.

Snell, M., & Brown, F. (2000). *Instruction of students with severe disabilities* (5th ed.). Upper Saddle River, NJ: Merrill/Prentice-Hall.

Snow, C., Burns, M., & Griffin, P. (1998). *Preventing reading difficulties in young children.* Washington, DC: National Academy Press.

Spradley, J. (1980). *Participant observation.* New York: Holt, Rinehart, & Winston.

Spring, J. (1997). *Political agendas for education: From the Christian coalition to the green party.* Mahwah, NJ: Lawrence Erlbaum Associates.

Stanovich, K. (1996). Word recognition: Changing perspectives. In R. Barr, M. Kamil, P. Mosenthal, & P. D. Pearson (Eds.), *Handbook of reading research: Volume II* (pp. 418–452). Mahwah, NJ: Lawrence Erlbaum Associates.

Strickland, D. (1998). *Teaching phonics today: A primer for educators.* Newark, DE: International Reading Association.

Strickland, R. G. (1964). The contribution of structural linguistics to the teaching of reading, writing, and grammar in the elementary school. *Bulleting of the School of Education, 40*(1). Bloomington: Indiana University.

Stuckey, J. E. (1991). *The violence of literacy.* Portsmouth, NH: Boynton/Cook.

Taylor, D. (1989, November). Toward a unified theory of literacy learning and instructional practice. *Phi Delta Kappan, 71*(3), 184–193.

Taylor, D. (1993). *From the child's point of view.* Portsmouth, NH: Heinemann.

Taylor, D. (1998). *Learning to read and the spin doctors of science: The political campaign to change America's mind about how children learn to read.* Urbana, IL: National Council of Teachers of English.

Templeton, S. (1995). *Children's literacy: Contexts for meaningful learning.* Boston: Houghton Mifflin.

Udell, R. (in prep.). *Untitled.* Unpublished doctoral dissertation, University of Nebraska–Lincoln.

Van Manen, M. (1986). *The tone of teaching.* Ontario: Scholastic.

Vellutino, F., & Denckla, M. (1996). Cognitive and neuropsychological foundations of word identification in poor and normally developing readers. In R. Barr, M. Kamil, P. Mosenthal, & P. D. Pearson (Eds.), *Handbook of reading research: Volume II* (pp. 571–608). Mahwah, NJ: Lawrence Erlbaum Associates.

Vernon, S., & Ferreiro, E. (1999, Winter). Writing development: A neglected variable in the consideration of phonological awareness. *Harvard Educational Review, 69*(4), 395–415.

Weaver, C. (1988). *Reading process and practice: From socio-psycholinguistics to whole language.* Portsmouth, NH: Heinemann.

Weaver, C. (1994). *Reading process and practice: From socio-psycholinguistics to whole language* (2nd ed.). Portsmouth, NH: Heinemann.

Weaver, C. (1998). Toward a balanced approach to reading. In C. Weaver (Ed.), *Reconsidering a balanced approach to reading* (pp. 11–76). Urbana, IL: National Council of Teachers of English.

Weaver, C., Gillmeister-Krause, L., & Vento-Zogby, G. (1996). *Creating support for effective literacy education: Workshop materials and handouts.* Portsmouth, NH: Heinemann.

Wells, G. (1986). *The meaning makers: Children learning language and using language to learn.* Portsmouth, NH: Heinemann.

Wells, G. (1999). *Dialogic inquiry: Towards a sociocultural practice and theory of education.* New York: Cambridge University Press.

Wells, G., & Chang-Wells, G. L. (1992). *Constructing knowledge together.* Portsmouth, NH: Heinemann.

Whitehead, A. N. (1949). *The aims of education.* New York: Mentor Books.

Whitmore, K., & Crowell, C. (1994). *Inventing a classroom: Life in a bilingual, whole language learning community.* York, ME: Stenhouse.

Willis, A. (1997). Focus on research: Historical considerations. *Language Arts, 74*(5), 387–397.

Willis, A., & Harris, V. (2000). Political acts: Literacy learning and teaching. *Reading Research Quarterly, 35*(1), 72–88.

Wilson, L. (2000). The emperor's new education. *Language Arts, 77*(4), 333–334.

Wolcott, H. (1990). On seeking—and rejecting—validity in qualitative research. In E. Eisner & A. Peshkin (Eds.), *Qualitative inquiry in education: The continuing debate* (pp. 121–152). New York: Teachers College Press.

Wortman, R. (1991). *Authenticity.* Unpublished doctoral dissertation, University of Arizona, Tucson.

Author Index

A

Adams, M., 86
Allington, R., 2, 81, 84, 125, 126
Altwerger, B., 59, 109, 110, 122
Amaya-Williams, M., 65, 66
Angelou, M., 47, 60
Applebee, A. N., 96
Atwell, N., 6
Au, K., 103
Avery, C., 6, 70

B

Barnes, M., 92
Barone, D., 36
Barr, R., 35
Baylor, B., 94, 95
Belenky, M., 57, 106
Bell, D., 91
Berliner, D. C., 1, 78, 108, 113
Bever, T. G., 34
Biddle, B. J., 1, 78, 108, 113
Bird, B., 122, 128
Bird, J., 122, 128
Bird, L., 59
Bloome, D., 18
Bond, G., 88
Borko, H., 51
Bower, T. G., 34
Brady, J., 99

Braunger, J., 50
Bredekamp, S., 3
Brinkley, E., 122, 128
Brown, F., 64
Brown, J., 105
Brown, L., 3, 5, 56, 87, 107, 117, 133
Brueggeman, B. J., 48
Buchanan, E., 42
Burke, C., 23, 90
Burns, M., 86

C

Cambourne, B., 67, 98, 109
Campbell, P., 122, 128
Carbo, M., 1
Carini, P., 115
Casanova, U., 65
Cazden, C., 89
Chall, J., 1
Chang-Wells, G. L., 26
Clinchy, B., 57, 106
Clymer, T., 45, 46, 145, 146, 153
Cochran, D., 42
Cochran, O., 42
Cochran-Smith, M., 50
Cole, J., 14, 22
Coles, G., 2, 55, 78, 86
Coles, R., 75
Crowell, C., 50
Cunningham, J., 86

Subject Index

W

Washington, DC, 123
Whole language, 1–2
Whole Language Umbrella (WLU), 139
Writing, 19–20, 22–24

Y

Yes Is Better Than No (Baylor), 94–95
You Can Make a Difference: A Teacher's Guide to Political Action (Keresty/O'Leary/Wortley), 129–130